Green World Unveiled

Exploring the Diversity and Importance of Plants

Iris Gardenia

Green World Unveiled

Table of contents

Chapter 1: The Significance of Earth's Green Mantle

The Role of Plants in Earth's Ecosystems

The tapestry of life on Earth is intricately woven, with plants serving as the vibrant threads that connect various ecosystems. Their significance extends beyond the mere production of oxygen and the sustenance of herbivores; plants play a pivotal role in maintaining ecological balance, supporting biodiversity, and influencing global climate patterns. From the smallest moss clinging to a damp rock to towering redwoods that touch the sky, plants form the backbone of life on our planet.

The role of plants as primary producers is fundamental to their ecological importance. Through photosynthesis, plants convert sunlight into chemical energy, producing organic compounds that serve as food for various organisms. This process not only sustains the plant itself but also provides energy for herbivores, which in turn support carnivores, creating a complex web of life. In essence, plants are the keystone species upon which entire ecosystems depend. Their ability to harness the sun's energy and transform it into a usable form is a marvel of nature, driving the flow of energy and nutrients through the biosphere.

Beyond their role as energy producers, plants contribute to the stability and health of ecosystems in numerous ways. One of their most crucial functions is maintaining soil structure and fertility. Plant roots bind the soil, preventing erosion and promoting the retention of water and nutrients. In forests, the leaf litter that falls to the ground decomposes, enriching the soil with organic matter and fostering a rich community of microorganisms. These processes create a hospitable environment for other plants to grow and support a diverse array of life forms.

Plants also play a vital role in regulating the Earth's climate. Forests, in particular, act as carbon sinks, absorbing vast amounts of carbon dioxide from the atmosphere and storing it in their biomass. This process helps mitigate the effects of climate change by reducing the concentration of greenhouse gases. Additionally, plants release water vapor into the atmosphere through a process called transpiration, which contributes to cloud formation and influences weather patterns. The presence of vegetation can even moderate local climates by providing shade and reducing temperature extremes.

The interconnectedness of plants and animal life is exemplified by the myriad symbiotic relationships that have evolved over millennia. Pollination is one of the most well-known examples, where insects, birds, and other animals transfer pollen from one flower to another, enabling plants to reproduce. In return, these pollinators receive nectar or pollen as a food source. This mutually beneficial relationship is essential for the reproduction of many plant species and the survival of the pollinators themselves. Similarly, certain plants have formed partnerships with fungi and bacteria, known as mycorrhizae and nitrogen-fixing bacteria, respectively. These symbioses enhance nutrient uptake for the plant while providing the microorganisms with carbohydrates.

The importance of plants extends to their influence on biodiversity. Diverse plant communities create a variety of habitats and niches, supporting a wide range of animal species. The structural complexity of a forest, for example, offers numerous opportunities for different organisms to thrive, from canopy-dwelling birds to ground-foraging mammals and insects. The loss of plant diversity, therefore, can have cascading effects on entire ecosystems, leading to a decline in animal populations and a reduction in ecosystem services. civilization has long been intertwined with the plant kingdom. From the earliest agricultural practices to modern-day horticulture, plants have been a source of food, medicine, and materials. Ancient cultures revered plants for their healing properties, and many traditional remedies are still in use today. The cultivation of crops has shaped human societies, enabling the development of cities and the growth of populations. In recent times, the study of plants has led to advancements in fields such as pharmacology, biotechnology, and environmental science.

Despite their immense value, plants face numerous threats from human activities. Deforestation, habitat fragmentation, pollution, and climate change are among the most pressing challenges. The loss of plant species not only diminishes biodiversity but also undermines the resilience of ecosystems and their ability to provide essential services. Conservation efforts are critical to preserving the planet's green mantle and ensuring the continued survival of countless species, including our own.

The role of plants in Earth's ecosystems is a testament to the delicate balance of nature. Their ability to adapt and thrive in diverse environments has allowed life to flourish on our planet. As stewards of the Earth, it is our responsibility to protect and preserve this green mantle for future generations. By understanding the intricate relationships between plants and other organisms, we can appreciate the complexity and beauty of the natural world and work towards a sustainable future.

Historical Perspectives on Plant Diversity

The tapestry of plant diversity has been woven over millions of years, shaped by evolutionary pressures, climatic changes, and geological events. As we delve into the historical perspectives on plant diversity, the story unfolds, revealing a fascinating journey that mirrors the history of our planet itself. From the earliest photosynthetic organisms to the lush forests that carpet the Earth today, plants have undergone a remarkable transformation, adapting to shifting environments and paving the way for the rich biodiversity we see now.

The origins of plant life trace back to over 500 million years ago during the Cambrian period, a time when multicellular life began to flourish in the oceans. It was in these ancient seas that the first photosynthetic organisms, cyanobacteria, played a pivotal role in transforming Earth's atmosphere by producing oxygen. This monumental shift set the stage for the evolution of more complex life forms. As time progressed, the fossil record reveals the emergence of early land plants, which began their colonization of terrestrial environments during the Ordovician period. These pioneering species were simple and lacked the vascular tissues that characterize most modern plants, yet their arrival marked a significant turning point in Earth's ecological history.

The Devonian period, often referred to as the "Age of Plants," witnessed a dramatic diversification of plant life. It was during this time that vascular plants, equipped with specialized tissues for transporting water and nutrients, made their appearance. This adaptation allowed plants to grow taller and colonize new habitats, leading to the formation of the first forests. These ancient woodlands, dominated by towering lycophytes, ferns, and horsetails, played a crucial role in altering global climates by sequestering carbon dioxide and influencing weather patterns.

As the Carboniferous period unfolded, plant diversity continued to expand, giving rise to extensive coal-forming forests that thrived in the warm, humid climates of the time. The lush vegetation not only provided habitat and sustenance for a burgeoning variety of animal life but also laid down vast deposits of organic material that would eventually become coal. This era of prolific plant growth had profound implications for Earth's carbon cycle, as it led to a significant drawdown of atmospheric carbon dioxide and a subsequent cooling of the planet.

The advent of seed-bearing plants during the late Paleozoic era marked another pivotal moment in the history of plant diversity. Gymnosperms, such as conifers, cycads, and ginkgos, developed the ability to reproduce using seeds, a major evolutionary innovation that provided a reproductive advantage in a variety of environments. The resilience and adaptability of seed plants allowed them to dominate terrestrial ecosystems throughout the Mesozoic era, a time when dinosaurs roamed the Earth.

The rise of angiosperms, or flowering plants, during the Cretaceous period brought about a dramatic shift in plant diversity. The development of flowers and fruits enabled angiosperms to establish mutually beneficial relationships with pollinators and seed dispersers, such as insects and birds. This co-evolutionary partnership spurred a rapid diversification of flowering plants, leading to the rich array of plant species that populate the Earth today. The success of angiosperms can be attributed to their remarkable adaptability, as they evolved a wide range of forms and functions to thrive in diverse habitats.

Throughout history, plant diversity has been influenced by numerous factors, including continental drift, climatic fluctuations, and catastrophic events such as mass extinctions. The breakup of the supercontinent Pangaea during the Mesozoic era, for example, led to the isolation of plant populations and the evolution of distinct flora on different landmasses. Similarly, the cooling and drying trends of the Cenozoic era prompted the expansion of grasslands and the diversification of grasses, which became the dominant vegetation in many regions. activities have also played a significant role in shaping plant diversity, both positively and negatively. The domestication of plants for agriculture, which began around 10,000 years ago, led to the cultivation of crop species that have become staples in human diets worldwide. However, the expansion of agriculture and urbanization has also contributed to habitat loss and the decline of native plant species. The introduction of invasive species, pollution, and climate change pose additional threats to plant diversity, underscoring the need for conservation efforts to preserve the Earth's botanical heritage.

The historical perspectives on plant diversity offer valuable insights into the resilience and adaptability of plant life. Understanding the evolutionary journey of plants and the factors that have shaped their diversity is essential for appreciating the complexity and beauty of the natural world. As we face the challenges of the modern era, it is crucial to recognize the importance of preserving plant diversity, not only for the health of ecosystems but also for the well-being of future generations. The story of plant diversity is a testament to the enduring power of nature and the intricate connections that bind all living things.

The Interconnectedness of Plants and Climate

In the grand tapestry of Earth's ecosystems, plants and climate are inextricably intertwined, each influencing and being influenced by the other in a dynamic dance that has persisted for millennia. These interactions have shaped the planet into the life-sustaining haven it is today, with plants acting as both responders to and regulators of climate patterns. Understanding the interconnectedness of plants and climate reveals the profound impact this relationship has on global ecological stability and biodiversity.

The role of plants as climate regulators is primarily rooted in their ability to absorb carbon dioxide from the atmosphere during photosynthesis. This process not only produces oxygen, essential for the survival of aerobic organisms, but also serves as a natural mechanism for mitigating climate change. Plants, particularly trees and large forests, act as carbon sinks, sequestering carbon dioxide in their biomass and reducing the amount of this potent greenhouse gas in the atmosphere. This sequestration helps to moderate global temperatures and maintain climatic equilibrium. The Amazon rainforest, often referred to as the "lungs of the Earth," exemplifies this vital function, absorbing vast quantities of carbon dioxide and releasing oxygen.

Beyond carbon sequestration, plants influence climate through the process of transpiration. As plants release water vapor into the atmosphere, they contribute to cloud formation and precipitation patterns. This process plays a critical role in the water cycle, impacting local and regional climates. Forested areas, for example, are often associated with increased rainfall and humidity, creating microclimates that support diverse ecosystems. The cooling effect of transpiration also helps to moderate surface temperatures, providing a buffer against the extremes of climate change.

The relationship between plants and climate is not a one-way street; climate, in turn, exerts a significant influence on plant life. Temperature, precipitation, and seasonal variations dictate the distribution and diversity of plant species across the globe. Adaptations to specific climatic conditions have led to the proliferation of distinct plant communities, from the arid deserts of cacti and succulents to the lush tropical rainforests teeming with biodiversity.

These adaptations illustrate the resilience and versatility of plant life in the face of environmental challenges.

Climate change, however, is testing the limits of this resilience. Rising temperatures, altered precipitation patterns, and increased frequency of extreme weather events are placing unprecedented stress on plant ecosystems. Many species face the threat of extinction as their habitats shift and degrade. The loss of plant diversity has cascading effects on the entire biosphere, as plants form the foundation of food webs and provide critical ecosystem services, such as soil stabilization, water purification, and habitat for wildlife.

To address the challenges posed by climate change, conservation and restoration efforts are essential. Protecting existing forests and reforesting degraded areas can enhance carbon sequestration and restore the natural balance between plants and climate. Additionally, promoting biodiversity through the preservation of native plant species can increase ecosystem resilience, enabling plant communities to better withstand climatic fluctuations. Sustainable land management practices, such as agroforestry and permaculture, can also play a role in mitigating climate impacts by integrating trees and shrubs into agricultural systems, thereby enhancing carbon storage and soil health.

The interplay between plants and climate extends beyond ecological considerations, influencing human societies in profound ways. Agriculture, for example, is heavily reliant on stable climatic conditions for crop production. Changes in temperature and precipitation can disrupt food supply chains, impacting food security and economies worldwide. The cultivation of climate-resilient crops and the implementation of sustainable farming practices are crucial for adapting to changing climatic conditions and ensuring a stable food supply.

Moreover, the cultural and spiritual significance of plants is deeply rooted in human history. Many indigenous communities have long recognized the symbiotic relationship between plants and climate, incorporating traditional ecological knowledge into their land stewardship practices. These practices offer valuable insights into sustainable living and highlight the importance of respecting and preserving the natural world.

In exploring the interconnectedness of plants and climate, it becomes clear that the health of our planet is intricately linked to the vitality of its vegetation. As stewards of the Earth, we bear the responsibility of nurturing this relationship, recognizing that our actions have far-reaching consequences for both the environment and future generations. By fostering a deeper understanding of the complex interactions between plants and climate, we can work towards a more sustainable and harmonious coexistence with the natural world. The journey to safeguarding our planet requires collective effort, guided by the wisdom of nature and informed by the lessons of the past.

The Role of Plants in Human Civilization

Throughout the annals of human history, plants have been more than mere backdrops to the unfolding drama of civilization. They have been vital actors, shaping societies, economies, and cultures in profound and multifaceted ways. From the dawn of agriculture to the modern era of biotechnology, the role of plants in human civilization is a testament to their indispensable value and adaptability.

The story begins with the Neolithic Revolution, a pivotal moment when humans transitioned from nomadic hunter-gatherer lifestyles to settled agricultural communities. This shift was made possible by the domestication of plants, as early humans began cultivating crops such as wheat, barley, rice, and maize. These staple crops provided a reliable food source, allowing populations to grow and communities to flourish. The emergence of agriculture laid the foundation for the development of complex societies, as surplus food enabled the specialization of labor and the rise of trade.

Plants have not only sustained human populations but have also played a crucial role in the development of economies. The cultivation and trade of cash crops such as cotton, sugar, tea, and coffee have historically driven economic growth and global commerce. The spice trade, for instance, was a catalyst for exploration and the establishment of trade routes between East and West. The desire for exotic spices like cinnamon, nutmeg, and pepper spurred voyages that led to the discovery of new lands and the exchange of cultural and technological innovations.

Beyond their economic impact, plants have also been central to the advancement of medicine. For millennia, humans have relied on the healing properties of plants to treat ailments and maintain health. Ancient civilizations, such as the Egyptians, Greeks, and Chinese, documented the medicinal uses of plants in texts that continue to inform modern pharmacology. Many contemporary medicines, including aspirin, quinine, and morphine, have been derived from plant compounds. The exploration of plant-based remedies has led to countless discoveries and continues to fuel the search for new treatments and cures.

The cultural significance of plants is equally profound, as they have been woven into the fabric of human expression and belief systems. In various cultures, plants have served as symbols of life, death, fertility, and renewal. They have been used in rituals, ceremonies, and artistic representations, reflecting the deep connection between humans and the natural world. The lotus flower, for example, is a potent symbol of purity and enlightenment in Hindu and Buddhist traditions. Similarly, the olive branch is universally recognized as a symbol of peace and reconciliation.

In addition to their symbolic meanings, plants have played a practical role in shaping human environments. The construction of shelters, tools, and clothing has relied heavily on plant materials such as wood, bamboo, and fibers. The use of plants in architecture is exemplified by traditional structures like the thatched roofs of rural cottages and the bamboo houses of Southeast Asia. These plant-based materials offer sustainable and renewable solutions that have stood the test of time.

As human civilization has advanced, so too has our ability to manipulate plant life for various purposes. The advent of biotechnology has revolutionized agriculture, enabling the development of genetically modified crops that are resistant to pests, diseases, and environmental stresses. These innovations have the potential to increase food security and reduce the environmental impact of farming practices. However, they also raise ethical and ecological concerns, highlighting the need for careful consideration and regulation.

The role of plants in human civilization is not without its challenges. Deforestation, habitat loss, and climate change threaten the delicate balance between plants and the ecosystems they support. The destruction of forests for agriculture and urban development has led to the loss of biodiversity and the degradation of natural resources. The impact of human activities on plant life underscores the urgency of conservation efforts to preserve the rich diversity of plant species for future generations.

In addressing these challenges, sustainable practices and policies are essential. Agroforestry, permaculture, and organic farming are examples of approaches that integrate plants into agricultural systems while promoting ecological balance. These practices emphasize the importance of biodiversity and the responsible stewardship of natural resources. Urban greening initiatives, such as the creation of green spaces and the incorporation of green roofs, can also enhance the quality of life in cities while mitigating the effects of climate change.

The enduring relationship between plants and human civilization is a testament to the resilience and adaptability of both. As we look to the future, it is imperative to recognize the vital role that plants play in sustaining life on Earth. By fostering a deeper understanding of this relationship and embracing sustainable practices, we can ensure that plants continue to enrich human societies and contribute to a thriving planet. The journey of plants through human history is a reflection of our shared destiny, one that calls for cooperation, innovation, and respect for the natural world.

Key Concepts in Understanding Plant Importance

Understanding the importance of plants within Earth's ecosystems requires a comprehensive grasp of key concepts that highlight their multifaceted roles. These concepts reveal the intricate ways in which plants support life, maintain ecological balance, and contribute to the planet's overall health. By delving into these foundational ideas, we can appreciate the profound significance of plants and the need to preserve their diversity and vitality.

At the heart of plant importance is the concept of photosynthesis, a process that serves as the cornerstone of life on Earth. Through photosynthesis, plants capture sunlight and convert it into chemical energy, producing oxygen as a byproduct. This process not only sustains the plants themselves but also forms the basis of food chains, providing the energy necessary for the survival of herbivores and, subsequently, carnivores. The oxygen released during photosynthesis is crucial for the respiration of most living organisms, underscoring the vital role plants play in maintaining atmospheric balance and supporting life.

Plants are integral to the functioning of ecosystems, serving as primary producers that drive the flow of energy and nutrients. They form the base of food webs, supporting a diverse array of organisms, from insects and birds to mammals and humans. The concept of trophic levels helps to illustrate this relationship, with plants occupying the first level and providing sustenance for higher-level consumers. Understanding this hierarchy is essential for recognizing the interconnectedness of all living beings and the pivotal role plants play in sustaining biodiversity.

In addition to their role as primary producers, plants contribute to the stability and resilience of ecosystems through their influence on biogeochemical cycles. The carbon cycle, for instance, is heavily reliant on plants' ability to sequester carbon dioxide from the atmosphere and store it in their biomass. This process not only mitigates the effects of climate change but also regulates global temperatures. Similarly, the nitrogen cycle is supported by plants' interactions with nitrogen-fixing bacteria, which convert atmospheric nitrogen into a form usable by plants. These cycles illustrate the dynamic interplay between plants and their environment, highlighting their essential contributions to ecological health.

The concept of ecosystem services further emphasizes the importance of plants, as they provide a wide range of benefits that support human well-being. These services include provisioning services, such as food, fuel, and fiber; regulating services, such as climate regulation and water purification; supporting services, such as soil formation and nutrient cycling; and cultural services, such as recreation and spiritual enrichment. By valuing these services, we can better appreciate the myriad ways in which plants enhance our lives and the necessity of conserving them for future generations.

Plants exhibit a remarkable ability to adapt to diverse environments, a concept that underscores their resilience and evolutionary success. This adaptability is evident in the wide range of morphological, physiological, and reproductive strategies that plants have developed to thrive in various habitats. Desert plants, for example, have evolved mechanisms to conserve water and withstand extreme temperatures, while aquatic plants have adapted to life in waterlogged conditions. These adaptations not only ensure the survival of individual species but also contribute to the richness of biodiversity within ecosystems.

The importance of plants is also reflected in their role as keystone species, organisms that have a disproportionately large impact on their environment relative to their abundance. Keystone plants, such as certain tree species, provide critical habitat and resources for a wide variety of organisms, shaping the structure and function of ecosystems. The loss of a keystone plant species can have cascading effects, leading to the decline of dependent species and the disruption of ecological balance. activities have increasingly impacted plant importance, presenting both challenges and opportunities for conservation. Urbanization, deforestation, and pollution have led to habitat loss and the decline of plant populations, threatening biodiversity and ecosystem services. However, human ingenuity also offers solutions, such as sustainable land management practices and conservation efforts that aim to protect and restore plant diversity. By recognizing the vital contributions of plants and implementing strategies to preserve them, we can ensure the continued health and resilience of Earth's ecosystems.

Education and awareness are crucial components in understanding and promoting the importance of plants. By fostering a deeper appreciation for the complexity and beauty of plant life, individuals and communities can be inspired to take action in support of conservation efforts. This awareness can lead to more informed decisions regarding land use, resource management, and environmental policies, ultimately contributing to a more sustainable and harmonious relationship with the natural world.

In exploring these key concepts, it becomes clear that plants are not merely passive components of ecosystems but active participants that shape the environment and support life. Their importance extends beyond their immediate ecological roles, influencing global processes and human societies in profound ways. By recognizing and valuing the contributions of plants, we can work towards a future that honors their significance and ensures their preservation for generations to come. The journey to understanding plant importance is one of discovery and stewardship, a path that invites us to embrace the interconnectedness of all life and the vital role that plants play in the tapestry of existence.

Chapter 2: The Rich Diversity of the Plant Kingdom

Major Plant Groups and Their Characteristics

Plants, the silent architects of our world, are categorized into several major groups, each distinguished by unique characteristics that define their roles in ecosystems. From the simplest non-vascular plants to the complex flowering angiosperms, the diversity of plant life showcases an evolutionary journey marked by adaptation and resilience.

The journey begins with bryophytes, a group comprising mosses, liverworts, and hornworts. As non-vascular plants, bryophytes lack specialized tissues for transporting water and nutrients, relying instead on their ability to absorb moisture directly from the environment. This limitation confines them to moist habitats, where they play crucial roles in water retention and soil formation. Despite their simplicity, bryophytes are remarkably resilient, often colonizing harsh environments such as rocky outcrops and nutrient-poor soils. Their lifecycle is dominated by the gametophyte stage, a characteristic that sets them apart from more complex plant groups.

Transitioning to more advanced vascular plants, we encounter pteridophytes, which include ferns and their relatives. Pteridophytes possess vascular tissues, xylem and phloem, that enable efficient water and nutrient transport, allowing them to grow taller and thrive in a wider range of environments. Ferns, with their characteristic fronds and spore-producing structures called sori, are a familiar sight in both temperate and tropical regions. Unlike bryophytes, the sporophyte stage dominates the lifecycle of pteridophytes, reflecting an evolutionary advancement in plant reproduction.

The development of seeds marks a significant evolutionary leap in the plant kingdom, giving rise to gymnosperms and angiosperms. Gymnosperms, such as conifers, cycads, and ginkgos, are characterized by their "naked seeds," which are not enclosed within a fruit. These plants are well-adapted to diverse climates, from the cold boreal forests of the Northern Hemisphere to the arid landscapes of the Southern Hemisphere. Conifers, with their needle-like leaves and cone-bearing reproductive structures, are particularly noteworthy for their ecological and economic importance. They dominate large swathes of forested land, providing habitat for wildlife and resources for human use.

The most diverse and ecologically successful group of plants is the angiosperms, or flowering plants. With over 300,000 species, angiosperms display an astonishing variety of forms and adaptations. Their defining feature is the flower, a complex reproductive structure that facilitates pollination and seed dispersal. Flowers attract a myriad of pollinators, from bees and butterflies to birds and bats, through vivid colors, enticing scents, and sweet nectars. This intricate relationship between angiosperms and pollinators has driven the co-evolution of both, resulting in the remarkable diversity of flowering plants.

Angiosperms are further divided into two main classes: monocots and dicots. Monocots, such as grasses, lilies, and orchids, are characterized by a single cotyledon, parallel-veined leaves, and floral parts in multiples of three. Their fibrous root systems and ability to grow in dense clusters make them well-suited to a variety of habitats, from open grasslands to dense tropical forests. Dicots, on the other hand, possess two cotyledons, net-veined leaves, and floral parts in multiples of four or five. This group includes a wide range of plants, from towering trees to delicate herbs, each adapted to specific ecological niches.

The success of angiosperms is also attributed to their fruit-bearing capabilities, which enhance seed dispersal. Fruits, the mature ovaries of flowers, come in countless forms, from fleshy berries to hard nuts, each adapted to different dispersal strategies. Some fruits are designed to be eaten by animals, while others utilize wind, water, or mechanical means to spread their seeds. This adaptability in seed dispersal contributes to the widespread distribution and ecological dominance of flowering plants.

The significance of these major plant groups extends beyond their ecological roles. They have shaped human history and culture, providing food, medicine, materials, and inspiration for countless generations. The cultivation of cereal crops, such as wheat, rice, and corn, has been fundamental to the development of civilizations, while the therapeutic properties of plants like willow, from which aspirin is derived, have advanced medicine. The aesthetic beauty of flowering plants has inspired art, literature, and horticulture, enriching human lives in myriad ways.

As we navigate the challenges of the modern world, understanding the characteristics and importance of major plant groups is crucial for conservation and sustainable development. The loss of plant diversity poses significant risks to ecosystems and human well-being, as plants provide essential services such as carbon sequestration, soil stabilization, and air purification. Preserving the rich tapestry of plant life requires concerted efforts to protect natural habitats, promote sustainable practices, and raise awareness of the vital roles plants play in our lives.

By appreciating the diversity and complexity of plant groups, we can foster a deeper connection with the natural world and recognize our responsibility to safeguard it. The story of plants is a testament to the power of adaptation and the resilience of life, offering valuable lessons as we strive to build a sustainable future for all. Each plant group, with its unique characteristics and contributions, is a vital thread in the fabric of life, weaving together the intricate web of Earth's ecosystems.

The Evolutionary Pathways of Plant Life

The story of plant evolution is a remarkable journey through time, an unfolding narrative of adaptation, survival, and transformation. It is a tale that stretches back over 500 million years, beginning in the primordial seas and extending to the lush forests and sprawling grasslands that cover the Earth today. This evolutionary saga is marked by key innovations that have enabled plants to colonize diverse environments, overcome challenges, and become the foundation of terrestrial ecosystems.

The earliest chapter in the history of plant life begins in the ancient oceans, where simple photosynthetic organisms, akin to modern-day cyanobacteria, began harnessing sunlight to produce energy. These early pioneers played a critical role in shaping Earth's atmosphere, releasing oxygen as a byproduct of photosynthesis and setting the stage for the evolution of more complex life forms. The presence of oxygen allowed for the development of aerobic organisms, paving the way for the rich tapestry of biodiversity that would follow.

From these humble beginnings, the first true plants emerged during the Ordovician period, approximately 470 million years ago. These early land plants, resembling today's liverworts and mosses, were non-vascular, lacking specialized tissues for transporting water and nutrients. Despite their simplicity, they represented a significant evolutionary leap, as they adapted to life on land and began to modify the Earth's landscape. Their presence contributed to soil formation and created new habitats for other organisms.

The Devonian period, often referred to as the "Age of Plants," witnessed a dramatic diversification of plant life. This era saw the rise of vascular plants, which possessed xylem and phloem tissues that allowed for efficient transport of water and nutrients. This innovation enabled plants to grow taller, paving the way for the development of the first forests. These ancient woodlands, dominated by towering ferns, horsetails, and lycophytes, played a crucial role in altering Earth's climate by sequestering carbon dioxide and influencing weather patterns.

The Carboniferous period marked another pivotal moment in plant evolution. During this time, extensive swampy forests flourished, laying down vast deposits of organic material that would eventually become coal. The lush vegetation of this era supported a diverse array of animal life and contributed to a significant drawdown of atmospheric carbon dioxide, leading to a cooling of the planet. The evolution of seed-bearing plants, or gymnosperms, further expanded the range of habitats that plants could colonize, as seeds provided a reproductive advantage in varied environments.

The subsequent rise of angiosperms, or flowering plants, during the Cretaceous period brought about a dramatic shift in plant diversity. Flowers, with their intricate structures and vivid colors, facilitated new modes of reproduction by attracting pollinators such as insects, birds, and mammals. This co-evolutionary relationship between angiosperms and their pollinators led to a rapid diversification of flowering plants, resulting in the vast array of species that populate the Earth today. The development of fruits, which aid in seed dispersal, further contributed to the success of angiosperms by enabling them to colonize new areas and establish themselves in varied ecosystems.

Throughout their evolutionary history, plants have demonstrated remarkable resilience and adaptability. They have survived mass extinctions, climatic shifts, and geological upheavals, continually evolving new strategies to thrive in changing environments. This adaptability is evident in the wide range of morphological, physiological, and reproductive traits that plants have developed, allowing them to occupy diverse ecological niches.

The evolutionary pathways of plant life are not just a testament to the resilience of plants but also an integral part of the story of life on Earth. Plants have shaped the planet's atmosphere, influenced the climate, and provided the foundation for complex ecosystems. Their evolution has been closely intertwined with that of animals, fungi, and other organisms, highlighting the interconnectedness of all life forms.

In the face of modern challenges such as climate change, habitat loss, and biodiversity decline, understanding the evolutionary history of plants is more important than ever.

This knowledge provides valuable insights into the mechanisms of adaptation and resilience, informing conservation efforts and guiding strategies for preserving plant diversity. By studying the evolutionary pathways of plant life, we can better appreciate the complexity and beauty of the natural world and recognize the vital role that plants play in sustaining life on Earth.

The journey of plant evolution is a story of innovation and transformation, a testament to the enduring power of nature to adapt and thrive. As we look to the future, it is essential to honor this legacy by safeguarding the rich diversity of plant life that has evolved over millions of years. The evolutionary pathways of plants offer valuable lessons in resilience and interconnectedness, reminding us of our shared responsibility to protect the planet and its myriad life forms.

Biodiversity Hotspots and Unique Flora

The story of plant evolution is a remarkable journey through time, an unfolding narrative of adaptation, survival, and transformation. It is a tale that stretches back over 500 million years, beginning in the primordial seas and extending to the lush forests and sprawling grasslands that cover the Earth today. This evolutionary saga is marked by key innovations that have enabled plants to colonize diverse environments, overcome challenges, and become the foundation of terrestrial ecosystems.

The earliest chapter in the history of plant life begins in the ancient oceans, where simple photosynthetic organisms, akin to modern-day cyanobacteria, began harnessing sunlight to produce energy. These early pioneers played a critical role in shaping Earth's atmosphere, releasing oxygen as a byproduct of photosynthesis and setting the stage for the evolution of more complex life forms. The presence of oxygen allowed for the development of aerobic organisms, paving the way for the rich tapestry of biodiversity that would follow.

From these humble beginnings, the first true plants emerged during the Ordovician period, approximately 470 million years ago. These early land plants, resembling today's liverworts and mosses, were non-vascular, lacking specialized tissues for transporting water and nutrients. Despite their simplicity, they represented a significant evolutionary leap, as they adapted to life on land and began to modify the Earth's landscape. Their presence contributed to soil formation and created new habitats for other organisms.

The Devonian period, often referred to as the "Age of Plants," witnessed a dramatic diversification of plant life. This era saw the rise of vascular plants, which possessed xylem and phloem tissues that allowed for efficient transport of water and nutrients. This innovation enabled plants to grow taller, paving the way for the development of the first forests. These ancient woodlands, dominated by towering ferns, horsetails, and lycophytes, played a crucial role in altering Earth's climate by sequestering carbon dioxide and influencing weather patterns.

The Carboniferous period marked another pivotal moment in plant evolution. During this time, extensive swampy forests flourished, laying down vast deposits of organic material that would eventually become coal. The lush vegetation of this era supported a diverse array of animal life and contributed to a significant drawdown of atmospheric carbon dioxide, leading to a cooling of the planet. The evolution of seed-bearing plants, or gymnosperms, further expanded the range of habitats that plants could colonize, as seeds provided a reproductive advantage in varied environments.

The subsequent rise of angiosperms, or flowering plants, during the Cretaceous period brought about a dramatic shift in plant diversity. Flowers, with their intricate structures and vivid colors, facilitated new modes of reproduction by attracting pollinators such as insects, birds, and mammals. This co-evolutionary relationship between angiosperms and their pollinators led to a rapid diversification of flowering plants, resulting in the vast array of species that populate the Earth today. The development of fruits, which aid in seed dispersal, further contributed to the success of angiosperms by enabling them to colonize new areas and establish themselves in varied ecosystems.

Throughout their evolutionary history, plants have demonstrated remarkable resilience and adaptability. They have survived mass extinctions, climatic shifts, and geological upheavals, continually evolving new strategies to thrive in changing environments. This adaptability is evident in the wide range of morphological, physiological, and reproductive traits that plants have developed, allowing them to occupy diverse ecological niches.

The evolutionary pathways of plant life are not just a testament to the resilience of plants but also an integral part of the story of life on Earth. Plants have shaped the planet's atmosphere, influenced the climate, and provided the foundation for complex ecosystems. Their evolution has been closely intertwined with that of animals, fungi, and other organisms, highlighting the interconnectedness of all life forms.

In the face of modern challenges such as climate change, habitat loss, and biodiversity decline, understanding the evolutionary history of plants is more important than ever. This knowledge provides valuable insights into the mechanisms of adaptation and resilience, informing conservation efforts and guiding strategies for preserving plant diversity. By studying the evolutionary pathways of plant life, we can better appreciate the complexity and beauty of the natural world and recognize the vital role that plants play in sustaining life on Earth.

The journey of plant evolution is a story of innovation and transformation, a testament to the enduring power of nature to adapt and thrive. As we look to the future, it is essential to honor this legacy by safeguarding the rich diversity of plant life that has evolved over millions of years. The evolutionary pathways of plants offer valuable lessons in resilience and interconnectedness, reminding us of our shared responsibility to protect the planet and its myriad life forms.

Endemic and Rare Plant Species

The world of plants is as diverse as it is vast, populated by countless species that have adapted to every conceivable environment on Earth. Among these are the endemic and rare plant species, which hold a special place in the tapestry of biodiversity. Endemic plants, by definition, are species that occur naturally in a particular region and nowhere else. These plants have evolved unique characteristics that enable them to thrive in their specific habitats, often forming the backbone of local ecosystems. Rare plant species, on the other hand, are those with small populations or limited distributions, often due to environmental or anthropogenic pressures.

Endemic plants are crucial to the ecological identity of their regions. Consider the giant sequoias of California, towering sentinels that have stood for thousands of years. These majestic trees are not only a symbol of the Sierra Nevada but also play a critical role in their ecosystem, providing habitat and food for a myriad of species. Their unique adaptations, such as fire-resistant bark and cones that release seeds in response to heat, illustrate the intricate ways in which endemic plants have evolved to fit their environments.

The fynbos of South Africa offers another example of endemic richness, home to over 9,000 plant species, 70% of which are found nowhere else. This biodiversity hotspot is characterized by a unique Mediterranean climate, with nutrient-poor soils that have driven plants to develop distinctive adaptations such as proteoid roots and specialized pollination relationships. The fynbos is a testament to the evolutionary creativity that endemic species can exhibit, resulting in an array of forms and functions that contribute to the resilience of the ecosystem.

Rare plant species, though not necessarily endemic, often share the characteristic of vulnerability. The reasons for rarity are varied and complex, ranging from specific habitat requirements to historical population declines. The ghost orchid of the Florida Everglades, with its ethereal blooms and elusive nature, is one such species. Its rarity is due in part to its dependence on a delicate balance of swampy conditions and the presence of specific mycorrhizal fungi necessary for its growth. This intricate relationship highlights the fragility and interconnectedness of rare plant species within their ecosystems.

Conservation of endemic and rare plants is of paramount importance, not only for the preservation of biodiversity but also for the ecosystem services these plants provide. They can play a role in soil stabilization, water filtration, and carbon sequestration, as well as support for pollinators and other wildlife. Moreover, they are valuable genetic reservoirs that may hold the keys to future agricultural or medicinal breakthroughs.

Efforts to protect these plants often involve addressing the threats they face. Habitat destruction, driven by urbanization, agriculture, and resource extraction, is a primary threat. Climate change also poses significant risks, as shifts in temperature and precipitation patterns can alter habitats beyond the tolerance of these specialized plants. Invasive species further exacerbate the situation, competing for resources and sometimes directly preying on native flora.

To safeguard these botanical treasures, conservationists employ a variety of strategies. In situ conservation focuses on protecting plants within their natural habitats, often through the establishment of protected areas or reserves. These areas serve as sanctuaries where plants can thrive without the pressures of human encroachment. Ex situ conservation, on the other hand, involves the preservation of plants outside their natural habitats, such as in botanical gardens or seed banks. This approach provides a safety net, ensuring that genetic material is preserved even if wild populations are lost.

Community involvement is another critical component of conservation efforts. By engaging local populations and raising awareness of the importance of endemic and rare plants, conservation programs can build support for sustainable practices and foster a sense of stewardship. Ecotourism, when managed responsibly, can also provide economic incentives for the protection of these species, turning natural resources into valuable assets for local communities.

In addition to conservation efforts, scientific research plays a vital role in understanding and preserving endemic and rare plants. Studies on plant physiology, genetics, and ecology can provide insights into the specific needs and vulnerabilities of these species, informing management strategies and helping to predict how they might respond to environmental changes. Collaboration between researchers, conservationists, and policymakers is essential to developing effective, science-based approaches to plant conservation.

The story of endemic and rare plants is one of both wonder and urgency. These species represent the incredible diversity and adaptability of life on Earth, each with its own unique place in the web of life. Yet, they are also among the most threatened, facing challenges that require immediate and concerted action. By protecting these plants, we not only preserve our planet's natural heritage but also maintain the ecological processes that sustain all life.

In the grand narrative of biodiversity, endemic and rare plants are chapters filled with intrigue, beauty, and lessons of resilience. They remind us of the complexities of nature and the delicate balance that must be maintained to ensure the health of ecosystems worldwide. As stewards of the Earth, it is our responsibility to cherish and protect these botanical rarities, ensuring that their stories continue to unfold for generations to come. The future of these plants is intertwined with our own, a shared journey towards a world where diversity is celebrated, and nature's wonders are preserved.

The Impact of Evolution on Plant Adaptations

The evolution of plants is a saga filled with challenges and triumphs, marked by an extraordinary array of adaptations that have allowed them to conquer every corner of the Earth. This evolutionary journey has spanned millions of years, resulting in a dazzling diversity of forms and functions. Each adaptation tells a story of survival, a testament to the resilience and ingenuity of plant life as it responds to the ever-changing environment.

One of the most fundamental adaptations in plant evolution is photosynthesis, the process by which plants convert sunlight into energy. This innovation not only sustains the plants themselves but also forms the bedrock of life on Earth, providing the primary energy source for nearly all ecosystems. The evolution of photosynthetic pathways, such as C3, C4, and CAM, illustrates the adaptability of plants to different environmental conditions. C4 photosynthesis, for instance, allows certain plants like maize and sugarcane to thrive in hot, arid environments by efficiently capturing carbon dioxide, minimizing water loss, and maximizing energy production.

The transition from aquatic to terrestrial life posed significant challenges for early plants, necessitating adaptations to cope with the harsh conditions of the land. The development of a robust cuticle, a waxy layer covering the plant's surface, was a crucial adaptation that minimized water loss and protected against desiccation. The evolution of stomata, small pores on the surface of leaves, enabled plants to regulate gas exchange, balancing the need for carbon dioxide uptake with the risk of water loss.

As plants colonized the land, the evolution of vascular tissues marked another pivotal adaptation. Xylem and phloem allowed for the efficient transport of water, nutrients, and sugars throughout the plant, enabling them to grow larger and access sunlight more effectively. This advancement paved the way for the development of trees and forests, transforming the landscape and providing new habitats for a myriad of organisms.

Reproductive adaptations have also played a significant role in plant evolution, enabling plants to diversify and occupy a wide range of ecological niches. The evolution of seeds was a transformative adaptation, providing a protective environment for the developing embryo and a nutrient reserve to support early growth. Seeds allowed plants to disperse over long distances and colonize new areas, increasing their resilience to environmental fluctuations.

The advent of flowers in angiosperms represented a major leap in plant reproductive strategies. Flowers facilitated intricate relationships with pollinators, such as insects, birds, and mammals, through diverse forms, colors, and scents. These co-evolutionary partnerships enhanced the efficiency of pollination and increased genetic diversity, contributing to the rapid diversification and success of flowering plants.

In addition to reproductive innovations, plants have evolved a plethora of structural adaptations to survive in diverse habitats. The development of thorns, spines, and prickles provides defense against herbivores, deterring animals from feeding on the plant's tender tissues. In arid environments, succulent plants have evolved thick, fleshy leaves or stems to store water, enabling them to withstand prolonged periods of drought.

Plants have also developed chemical adaptations, producing a vast array of secondary metabolites that serve as defense mechanisms against herbivores, pathogens, and competitors. Alkaloids, terpenes, and phenolics are just a few examples of these compounds, which can deter herbivory, inhibit microbial growth, or allelopathically suppress the growth of neighboring plants. These chemical defenses highlight the complex interactions between plants and their environment, as well as the ongoing evolutionary arms race between plants and their adversaries.

The impact of evolution on plant adaptations is also evident in their ability to respond to environmental cues and stresses. Tropisms, such as phototropism and gravitropism, allow plants to orient their growth towards light or in response to gravity, optimizing their chances for survival and reproduction. Plants have also evolved complex signaling pathways to perceive and respond to environmental changes, such as drought, temperature fluctuations, and pathogen attacks. These responses can involve changes in gene expression, physiology, and morphology, illustrating the dynamic nature of plant adaptation. activity has introduced new challenges for plants, prompting further evolutionary responses. Urbanization, pollution, and climate change have created novel environments that require plants to adapt rapidly or face extinction. Some plants have developed tolerance to heavy metals or pollutants, while others have shifted their flowering times in response to changing climate patterns. These adaptations underscore the resilience of plants and their capacity to evolve in the face of unprecedented pressures.

Understanding the impact of evolution on plant adaptations provides valuable insights into the resilience and ingenuity of plant life. It highlights the importance of preserving plant diversity, as each species represents a unique solution to the challenges of survival. By studying plant adaptations, we can gain a deeper appreciation for the complexity of nature and the delicate balance that sustains life on Earth.

The story of plant evolution is a testament to the power of adaptation and the relentless drive for survival. It reminds us of the interconnectedness of all living things and the intricate web of life that binds us together. As we continue to explore the wonders of plant adaptations, we are reminded of our responsibility to protect and preserve the natural world, ensuring that the legacy of plant evolution endures for future generations. The journey of plants is a story of resilience and innovation, a testament to the enduring power of life to adapt and thrive in an ever-changing world.

Chapter 3: Plant Anatomy and Functional Adaptations

Cellular Structures and Their Roles

The evolution of plants is a saga filled with challenges and triumphs, marked by an extraordinary array of adaptations that have allowed them to conquer every corner of the Earth. This evolutionary journey has spanned millions of years, resulting in a dazzling diversity of forms and functions. Each adaptation tells a story of survival, a testament to the resilience and ingenuity of plant life as it responds to the ever-changing environment.

One of the most fundamental adaptations in plant evolution is photosynthesis, the process by which plants convert sunlight into energy. This innovation not only sustains the plants themselves but also forms the bedrock of life on Earth, providing the primary energy source for nearly all ecosystems. The evolution of photosynthetic pathways, such as C3, C4, and CAM, illustrates the adaptability of plants to different environmental conditions. C4 photosynthesis, for instance, allows certain plants like maize and sugarcane to thrive in hot, arid environments by efficiently capturing carbon dioxide, minimizing water loss, and maximizing energy production.

The transition from aquatic to terrestrial life posed significant challenges for early plants, necessitating adaptations to cope with the harsh conditions of the land. The development of a robust cuticle, a waxy layer covering the plant's surface, was a crucial adaptation that minimized water loss and protected against desiccation. The evolution of stomata, small pores on the surface of leaves, enabled plants to regulate gas exchange, balancing the need for carbon dioxide uptake with the risk of water loss.

As plants colonized the land, the evolution of vascular tissues marked another pivotal adaptation. Xylem and phloem allowed for the efficient transport of water, nutrients, and sugars throughout the plant, enabling them to grow larger and access sunlight more effectively. This advancement paved the way for the development of trees and forests, transforming the landscape and providing new habitats for a myriad of organisms.

Reproductive adaptations have also played a significant role in plant evolution, enabling plants to diversify and occupy a wide range of ecological niches. The evolution of seeds was a transformative adaptation, providing a protective environment for the developing embryo and a nutrient reserve to support early growth. Seeds allowed plants to disperse over long distances and colonize new areas, increasing their resilience to environmental fluctuations.

The advent of flowers in angiosperms represented a major leap in plant reproductive strategies. Flowers facilitated intricate relationships with pollinators, such as insects, birds, and mammals, through diverse forms, colors, and scents. These co-evolutionary partnerships enhanced the efficiency of pollination and increased genetic diversity, contributing to the rapid diversification and success of flowering plants.

In addition to reproductive innovations, plants have evolved a plethora of structural adaptations to survive in diverse habitats. The development of thorns, spines, and prickles provides defense against herbivores, deterring animals from feeding on the plant's tender tissues. In arid environments, succulent plants have evolved thick, fleshy leaves or stems to store water, enabling them to withstand prolonged periods of drought.

Plants have also developed chemical adaptations, producing a vast array of secondary metabolites that serve as defense mechanisms against herbivores, pathogens, and competitors. Alkaloids, terpenes, and phenolics are just a few examples of these compounds, which can deter herbivory, inhibit microbial growth, or allelopathically suppress the growth of neighboring plants. These chemical defenses highlight the complex interactions between plants and their environment, as well as the ongoing evolutionary arms race between plants and their adversaries.

The impact of evolution on plant adaptations is also evident in their ability to respond to environmental cues and stresses. Tropisms, such as phototropism and gravitropism, allow plants to orient their growth towards light or in response to gravity, optimizing their chances for survival and reproduction. Plants have also evolved complex signaling pathways to perceive and respond to environmental changes, such as drought, temperature fluctuations, and pathogen attacks. These responses can involve changes in gene expression, physiology, and morphology, illustrating the dynamic nature of plant adaptation. activity has introduced new challenges for plants, prompting further evolutionary responses. Urbanization, pollution, and climate change have created novel environments that require plants to adapt rapidly or face extinction. Some plants have developed tolerance to heavy metals or pollutants, while others have shifted their flowering times in response to changing climate patterns. These adaptations underscore the resilience of plants and their capacity to evolve in the face of unprecedented pressures.

Understanding the impact of evolution on plant adaptations provides valuable insights into the resilience and ingenuity of plant life. It highlights the importance of preserving plant diversity, as each species represents a unique solution to the challenges of survival. By studying plant adaptations, we can gain a deeper appreciation for the complexity of nature and the delicate balance that sustains life on Earth.

The story of plant evolution is a testament to the power of adaptation and the relentless drive for survival. It reminds us of the interconnectedness of all living things and the intricate web of life that binds us together. As we continue to explore the wonders of plant adaptations, we are reminded of our responsibility to protect and preserve the natural world, ensuring that the legacy of plant evolution endures for future generations. The journey of plants is a story of resilience and innovation, a testament to the enduring power of life to adapt and thrive in an ever-changing world.

Root Systems and Nutrient Acquisition

Beneath the surface of the earth lies a hidden world, a complex network of roots that anchors plants and plays a crucial role in their survival. Root systems are vital for nutrient acquisition, providing the foundation upon which plants build their lives. Understanding root systems, their structures, and their functions can reveal the intricacies of how plants thrive and adapt to their environments.

Roots are the unsung heroes of the plant kingdom, working tirelessly to explore the soil, absorb nutrients, and provide stability. They come in various forms, each uniquely adapted to the conditions of their surroundings. At the core, there are two primary types of root systems: taproots and fibrous roots. Taproots, exemplified by the carrot, consist of a single, dominant root that grows deep into the soil, providing access to water and nutrients far below the surface. This type of root system is advantageous in arid environments, where moisture is scarce and often found deep underground.

In contrast, fibrous root systems are composed of numerous small roots that spread out widely in the soil, as seen in grasses. This network of roots is efficient at absorbing nutrients and water from the upper layers of soil, making it ideal for environments where resources are plentiful but competition is fierce. Fibrous roots also play an essential role in preventing soil erosion, as their extensive networks hold the soil together, protecting it from the forces of wind and water.

Root systems are not only about structure; they are also about strategy. Plants have evolved various mechanisms to enhance their nutrient acquisition capabilities. Root hairs, tiny extensions of root cells, increase the surface area available for absorption, allowing plants to tap into a larger volume of soil. Mycorrhizal associations, a symbiotic relationship between plant roots and fungi, further enhance nutrient uptake. The fungi extend the reach of the roots, accessing nutrients in the soil that the plant roots alone could not obtain. In return, the plant supplies the fungi with carbohydrates produced through photosynthesis. This mutualistic relationship is a testament to the cooperative nature of life, where different organisms work together to overcome the challenges of survival.

Nutrient acquisition is a complex process that involves the uptake of essential elements from the soil, such as nitrogen, phosphorus, and potassium. These nutrients are vital for various physiological functions, including growth, energy production, and reproduction. Plants have developed specialized transport proteins within their root cells to facilitate the movement of these nutrients from the soil into the plant. The efficiency of nutrient uptake is influenced by several factors, including soil pH, temperature, and moisture levels. For example, acidic soils can limit the availability of certain nutrients, prompting plants to adjust their root architecture or develop specialized adaptations to cope with such conditions.

Root systems are dynamic and responsive, constantly adjusting to the ever-changing environment. They can sense and respond to various stimuli, such as gravity, water availability, and nutrient concentrations. This ability to adapt is crucial for plants to optimize their growth and ensure their survival. In nutrient-poor soils, plants may develop longer or more branched roots to increase their reach and maximize nutrient acquisition. In waterlogged conditions, some plants can develop specialized structures called aerenchyma, which allow for the diffusion of oxygen to submerged roots, preventing suffocation and decay.

The study of root systems and nutrient acquisition is not only fascinating but also has practical applications.

Understanding how plants interact with their environment can inform agricultural practices, leading to more sustainable and efficient food production. Techniques such as crop rotation, cover cropping, and the use of organic fertilizers can enhance soil health and promote robust root development, ultimately improving crop yields and reducing the need for chemical inputs.

Moreover, the knowledge gained from studying root systems can contribute to environmental conservation efforts. By understanding how plants stabilize soil and prevent erosion, land management practices can be developed to protect vulnerable ecosystems and promote biodiversity. Additionally, the insights gained from plant-fungal interactions can be applied to restore degraded landscapes, as the reintroduction of beneficial mycorrhizal fungi can support the establishment of native plant species and accelerate ecosystem recovery.

Root systems are also a source of inspiration for technological innovation. The principles of nutrient acquisition and resource optimization observed in plants can be applied to the design of more efficient water and nutrient delivery systems in agriculture. Furthermore, the study of plant root architecture can inform the development of bio-inspired structures and materials, leading to advances in fields such as engineering and materials science.

As we delve deeper into the world of roots, we uncover the intricate relationships between plants and their environment. Root systems are a testament to the adaptability and resilience of life, showcasing the remarkable strategies that plants employ to survive and thrive. By understanding the complexities of root systems and nutrient acquisition, we gain valuable insights into the natural world and the interconnectedness of all living things.

In this hidden realm beneath our feet, roots weave a tapestry of life, connecting plants with the soil and shaping the landscapes we see. Their silent, relentless pursuit of nutrients and stability is a reminder of the ingenuity and persistence of nature. As stewards of the Earth, it is our responsibility to appreciate and protect the delicate balance that root systems help maintain, ensuring that future generations can continue to marvel at the wonders of the plant kingdom. Through the study and appreciation of root systems, we can foster a deeper connection with the natural world and work towards a more sustainable and harmonious coexistence with the environment.

Leaf Morphology and Photosynthetic Efficiency

Leaves are the quintessential powerhouses of the plant world, orchestrating the conversion of sunlight into energy through the process of photosynthesis. This remarkable ability is not merely a function of the leaf's internal machinery but is intricately linked to its morphology—the shape, size, and structure of the leaf. Leaf morphology influences photosynthetic efficiency, dictating how effectively a plant can harness the sun's energy and thrive in its environment.

The diversity of leaf shapes and sizes in the plant kingdom is staggering, each adaptation a response to the specific ecological demands faced by a species. Broad, flat leaves, like those of the maple tree, are designed to capture maximum sunlight, a vital adaptation for life in temperate forests where light filtering through the canopy can be scarce. These leaves often have a large surface area relative to their volume, increasing their ability to absorb sunlight and facilitating the exchange of gases necessary for photosynthesis.

In contrast, needle-like leaves, such as those found in conifers, are adapted to environments where water conservation is paramount. Their reduced surface area minimizes water loss through transpiration, making them well-suited for cold or arid climates. The thick, waxy cuticle that often accompanies needle-like leaves provides additional protection against water loss and harsh environmental conditions. Despite their small size, these leaves are highly efficient at photosynthesis, utilizing the available light and resources to sustain the plant's energy needs.

Leaf arrangement, or phyllotaxy, also plays a crucial role in optimizing photosynthetic efficiency. By positioning leaves in a spiral, alternate, or opposite pattern, plants can minimize shading of one leaf by another, ensuring that each leaf receives adequate sunlight. This strategic arrangement allows for efficient light capture while maintaining optimal spacing for gas exchange and nutrient distribution.

The internal structure of a leaf is equally important in determining photosynthetic efficiency. Within the leaf, the arrangement of cells and tissues is designed to maximize light absorption and the diffusion of gases. The mesophyll, the inner tissue of the leaf, contains chloroplasts—the organelles responsible for photosynthesis. Palisade mesophyll cells, which are elongated and densely packed, are arranged to capture light efficiently. Below them, the spongy mesophyll has a looser arrangement, creating air spaces that facilitate gas exchange.

Stomata, tiny pores on the leaf surface, are critical for gas exchange, allowing carbon dioxide to enter the leaf and oxygen to exit. The number, size, and distribution of stomata can greatly influence photosynthetic efficiency. In environments with ample water supply, plants may have more stomata to maximize gas exchange. However, in arid conditions, plants may reduce the number of stomata or develop mechanisms to close them during the hottest parts of the day to conserve water while still maintaining photosynthetic activity.

Leaf morphology is not static; it can change in response to environmental conditions. This plasticity allows plants to adapt to varying light levels, temperatures, and water availability. For instance, sun leaves, which develop in high light conditions, are often smaller and thicker, with more chloroplasts to optimize light capture and photosynthesis. In contrast, shade leaves are typically larger and thinner, maximizing surface area to capture diffuse light in shaded environments.

Photosynthetic pathways also influence leaf morphology and efficiency. C3 photosynthesis, the most common pathway, is efficient under cool, moist conditions with normal light intensity. C4 photosynthesis, found in plants like corn and sugarcane, is an adaptation to high light, high temperature environments. C4 plants have specialized anatomy, including the arrangement of bundle sheath cells, which allows them to concentrate carbon dioxide and reduce photorespiration, improving efficiency under these conditions. CAM photosynthesis, seen in succulents like cacti, allows plants to fix carbon dioxide at night, reducing water loss during the hot daytime hours.

The study of leaf morphology and photosynthetic efficiency is not only captivating but holds practical implications for agriculture and horticulture. By understanding how different leaf structures and arrangements contribute to photosynthesis, scientists and farmers can develop crops that are more efficient at converting sunlight into energy, leading to higher yields and more sustainable practices.

Additionally, the principles of leaf morphology can inform the design of artificial systems aimed at mimicking photosynthesis. By studying the natural adaptations of leaves, engineers and designers can develop more efficient solar panels and energy capture technologies, drawing inspiration from the elegant solutions found in nature.

Leaf morphology is a testament to the ingenious strategies plants employ to survive and thrive. Each leaf tells a story of adaptation, a narrative of evolution sculpted by the demands of the environment. Through the lens of leaf morphology, we gain insight into the complex interplay between form and function, a dance that has unfolded over millions of years.

The world of leaves is a microcosm of the broader ecological tapestry, a reminder of the intricate connections that bind all life. By appreciating the diversity and adaptability of leaf structures, we deepen our understanding of the natural world and our place within it. The lessons gleaned from the study of leaves extend beyond biology, offering inspiration and guidance for sustainable living and innovative design.

In the end, leaves are more than mere appendages of plants; they are symbols of life itself—resilient, adaptable, and endlessly fascinating. Their ability to capture sunlight and transform it into life-sustaining energy is a marvel of nature, a process that sustains the interconnected web of life on Earth. As we continue to explore and appreciate the wonders of leaf morphology, we reaffirm our commitment to preserving the delicate balance of the ecosystems that sustain us all.

Stem Architecture and Support Mechanisms

Stems are the structural backbone of plants, serving as the vital conduit for nutrients, water, and energy between the roots and leaves. Their architecture and support mechanisms are not merely feats of botanical engineering but are also pivotal to the plant's ability to thrive in diverse environments. The design of a stem reflects a plant's adaptation to its habitat, ensuring stability, resilience, and efficiency in resource allocation.

In the plant kingdom, stems exhibit a remarkable range of forms, each uniquely suited to its ecological niche. The towering trunks of trees like redwoods and oaks are the epitome of strength and durability, enabling these giants to reach for sunlight high above the forest floor. Their stems, composed of layers of tough lignin and cellulose, provide the necessary rigidity to support massive canopies and withstand the forces of wind and weather. The woody structure also facilitates the transport of water and nutrients from the roots to the extremities, maintaining the health and vitality of the entire organism.

Conversely, the slender, flexible stems of climbing plants like vines tell a different story of adaptation. These plants have evolved to use external structures for support, allowing them to reach sunlight without investing heavily in thick, self-supporting stems. Through specialized structures such as tendrils, hooks, or adhesive pads, climbers attach themselves to trees, walls, or other surfaces, deftly navigating their environment. This adaptation not only conserves energy and resources but also maximizes the plant's exposure to light, a clever strategy in densely vegetated areas.

Herbaceous plants, with their soft, flexible stems, often rely on turgor pressure for support. The cells within these stems are filled with water, creating internal pressure that keeps the plant upright. This reliance on water means that herbaceous plants are particularly sensitive to changes in hydration, wilting visibly when water is scarce. However, this system allows for rapid growth and flexibility, enabling these plants to quickly colonize open areas and respond to environmental changes.

The internal structure of plant stems is intricately designed to facilitate both support and transport. Vascular bundles, composed of xylem and phloem tissues, are the lifelines of the plant. Xylem vessels transport water and dissolved minerals from the roots upward, while phloem distributes the sugars produced during photosynthesis from the leaves to the rest of the plant. This dual transport system is vital for maintaining the plant's metabolic functions and supporting growth.

In addition to vascular tissues, stems may feature specialized cells that contribute to their strength and flexibility. Collenchyma cells, for example, provide support through their thickened cell walls, yet remain pliable enough to accommodate growth. Sclerenchyma cells, with their rigid, lignified walls, offer additional structural support, particularly in mature plants.

Stem architecture is not static; it can adapt to environmental conditions. For instance, in response to wind or mechanical stress, many plants exhibit a phenomenon known as thigmomorphogenesis, where stems grow thicker and stronger to better withstand such forces. This adaptive growth ensures that plants remain stable and upright, even in challenging conditions.

Beyond their structural roles, stems are also critical for reproduction and survival in certain species. Some plants propagate through stolons or rhizomes, horizontal stems that spread across or beneath the soil, respectively. These structures enable plants to colonize new areas and produce clones, ensuring the continuation of the species. In arid environments, some plants have evolved succulent stems capable of storing water, an adaptation that allows them to survive prolonged periods of drought.

The study of stem architecture and support mechanisms offers insights into the evolutionary strategies plants have developed to succeed in their respective habitats. These adaptations underscore the importance of form and function in the natural world, highlighting the intricate balance between growth, resource allocation, and environmental interaction.

For those interested in horticulture or agriculture, understanding stem architecture can inform practices that enhance plant health and productivity. Techniques such as pruning, staking, and training can be used to manipulate stem growth, improving light penetration, air circulation, and structural integrity of crops and ornamental plants. In forestry and conservation, knowledge of stem dynamics can aid in the management and restoration of ecosystems, ensuring the sustainability and resilience of plant communities.

Moreover, the principles of plant stem architecture inspire innovations in human engineering and design. The natural solutions evolved by plants to achieve strength, flexibility, and efficiency offer valuable lessons for creating sustainable and resilient structures in our built environment.

In essence, plant stems are a testament to the ingenuity of nature, embodying a complex interplay of physical forces and biological processes. Their architecture reflects the diverse strategies plants use to navigate their world, adapting to the challenges and opportunities presented by their surroundings.

By delving into the structural and functional aspects of stems, we gain a deeper appreciation for the resilience and adaptability of plant life. This understanding not only enhances our connection to the natural world but also equips us with the knowledge to support and preserve the myriad forms of life that depend on healthy and functioning ecosystems.

As we continue to explore the intricacies of stem architecture, we are reminded of the enduring power of evolution to shape life in all its complexity and diversity. The story of stems is one of innovation and survival, a narrative that spans millennia and continues to unfold in the landscapes around us. Through this lens, we see the remarkable capacity of plants to adapt, endure, and thrive—a source of inspiration and wonder in the ever-evolving tapestry of life.

Floral Structures and Reproductive Strategies

Floral structures are among the most captivating and diverse elements of the plant kingdom, dazzling us with their beauty while playing a crucial role in plant reproduction. These structures are not only aesthetically pleasing but are intricately designed to ensure the continuation of species. The variety of floral forms and reproductive strategies in plants is a testament to the evolutionary pressures they have faced and overcome.

At the core of plant reproduction lies the flower, a complex structure composed of several parts, each with a specific function. The sepals, often green and leaf-like, form the outermost layer, protecting the developing bud. Inside, the petals, with their vibrant colors and alluring scents, serve to attract pollinators such as bees, butterflies, and birds. These pollinators are essential partners in the reproductive process, facilitating the transfer of pollen from one flower to another.

Within the flower, the male reproductive organs, known as stamens, produce pollen, the carrier of male gametes. Each stamen consists of a filament and an anther, where pollen is produced and stored. In close proximity lie the female reproductive organs, called pistils, which typically consist of the stigma, style, and ovary. The stigma serves as a receptive surface for pollen, while the style provides a passageway to the ovary, where fertilization occurs and seeds develop.

The intricate dance of pollination and fertilization is central to the reproductive success of flowering plants. Various strategies have evolved to ensure the efficient transfer of pollen, each tailored to the plant's specific ecological niche. Some plants rely on wind or water to disperse their pollen, a strategy that requires the production of large quantities of pollen to increase the likelihood of successful pollination. Grasses and conifers are classic examples of wind-pollinated plants, with lightweight pollen grains that can travel great distances.

In contrast, many flowering plants have evolved to exploit the services of animals for pollination. These plants often produce showy flowers with enticing nectar rewards to attract pollinators. The relationship between plants and their pollinators can be highly specialized, with certain flowers adapted to be pollinated by specific species. The shape, size, and color of a flower can influence which pollinators visit, creating a dynamic interplay between plant and animal that drives both co-evolution and diversification.

The diversity of floral structures is matched by the array of reproductive strategies plants employ. Some plants are monoecious, bearing both male and female flowers on the same individual, while others are dioecious, with separate male and female plants. This separation can promote genetic diversity by encouraging cross-pollination between different individuals.

Self-pollination is another strategy used by some plants, offering the advantage of reproductive assurance when pollinators or mates are scarce. However, self-pollination can lead to inbreeding and reduced genetic variation, which may make plants more vulnerable to environmental changes and diseases. To mitigate this risk, many plants have developed mechanisms to promote outcrossing, such as self-incompatibility systems that prevent self-fertilization.

The fruits developed post-fertilization serve as protective vessels for seeds and play a crucial role in seed dispersal.

The structure and composition of fruits are as varied as the plants themselves, each adapted to specific dispersal methods. Fleshy fruits, like berries and apples, attract animals that consume the fruit and disperse the seeds through their droppings. Other fruits, like those of dandelions and maples, are designed for wind dispersal, with specialized structures that allow them to be carried over long distances.

Some plants have evolved explosive mechanisms to disperse their seeds, launching them away from the parent plant to reduce competition and increase the likelihood of colonizing new areas. These diverse strategies ensure that seeds are spread across a wide range of environments, increasing the chances of successful germination and growth.

Understanding floral structures and reproductive strategies is not only fascinating but also has practical applications. In agriculture and horticulture, knowledge of plant reproduction is essential for the cultivation and breeding of crops. Selective breeding, hybridization, and genetic modification are employed to produce plants with desirable traits, such as increased yield, disease resistance, or improved nutritional content.

Moreover, the preservation of pollinators and their habitats is critical for maintaining the health and productivity of ecosystems and agricultural systems. Pollinators are responsible for the reproduction of many food crops and wild plants, and their decline poses a significant threat to biodiversity and food security. Conservation efforts aimed at protecting pollinators, such as creating pollinator-friendly habitats and reducing pesticide use, are essential for sustaining the intricate web of life that depends on these vital organisms.

In the realm of ecological restoration and conservation, understanding plant reproductive strategies can inform the management and recovery of degraded ecosystems. By selecting plant species with compatible pollination and dispersal mechanisms, restoration practitioners can enhance the resilience and diversity of restored habitats.

Floral structures and reproductive strategies are a testament to the ingenuity of nature, showcasing the myriad ways plants have adapted to their environments to ensure their survival and reproduction. Through the lens of plant reproduction, we gain a deeper appreciation for the complexity and beauty of the natural world, as well as the interconnectedness of all life forms.

The study of plant reproduction also provides valuable insights into the evolutionary processes that have shaped the diversity of life on Earth. By examining the relationships between plants and their pollinators, dispersers, and habitats, we uncover the intricate networks of interaction that drive evolution and sustain ecosystems.

As we continue to explore the wonders of floral structures and reproductive strategies, we are reminded of the importance of preserving the delicate balance of nature. By protecting the diversity of plant life and their pollinators, we ensure the continued vitality of the ecosystems that sustain us all. The story of plant reproduction is one of resilience and adaptation, a narrative that inspires and informs our efforts to live in harmony with the natural world.

Chapter 4: The Ecological Roles of Plants

Plants as Primary Producers in Ecosystems

Floral structures captivate with their beauty and intricacy, playing a central role in the reproductive success of plants. Each flower is a masterpiece of evolution, designed to attract pollinators and ensure the continuation of the species. This diversity in form and function is a testament to the various ecological pressures plants have adapted to over time.

At the heart of plant reproduction is the flower, a complex structure with several parts, each serving a distinct purpose. The sepals, often green and protective, form the outermost layer, safeguarding the developing bud. Inside, vivid petals entice pollinators such as bees, butterflies, and birds with their colors and scents. These pollinators are essential partners, facilitating the transfer of pollen from one flower to another, thus enabling fertilization.

The male reproductive organs, or stamens, produce pollen, which carries the male gametes. Each stamen is composed of a filament and an anther, where pollen is produced and stored. Nearby, the female reproductive organs, known as pistils, consist of the stigma, style, and ovary. The stigma acts as a landing pad for pollen, while the style provides a pathway to the ovary, where fertilization and seed development occur.

Pollination and fertilization are crucial for flowering plants. Various strategies have evolved to ensure effective pollen transfer, each tailored to a plant's ecological niche. Wind and water are common agents of pollen dispersal for plants producing large quantities of pollen, like grasses and conifers. These plants rely on lightweight pollen that can travel long distances, maximizing the chances of successful pollination.

In contrast, many flowering plants have evolved to use animals for pollination. These plants produce showy flowers with nectar rewards to attract pollinators. The relationship between plants and their pollinators can be highly specialized, with flowers adapted to attract specific species. The shape, size, and color of a flower influence which pollinators visit, creating a dynamic interplay between plant and animal that drives co-evolution and diversification.

Floral structures and reproductive strategies are as diverse as the plants themselves. Some plants are monoecious, bearing both male and female flowers on the same individual, while others are dioecious, with separate male and female plants. This separation can promote genetic diversity by encouraging cross-pollination between different individuals.

Self-pollination is another strategy used by some plants, offering reproductive assurance when pollinators or mates are scarce. However, self-pollination can lead to inbreeding and reduced genetic variation, making plants more vulnerable to environmental changes and diseases. To mitigate this risk, many plants have developed mechanisms to promote outcrossing, such as self-incompatibility systems that prevent self-fertilization.

Following fertilization, fruits develop as protective vessels for seeds and play a crucial role in seed dispersal. The structure and composition of fruits are as varied as the plants themselves, each adapted to specific dispersal methods. Fleshy fruits, like berries and apples, attract animals that consume the fruit and disperse the seeds through their droppings. Other fruits, such as those of dandelions and maples, are designed for wind dispersal, with specialized structures that allow them to be carried over long distances.

Some plants have evolved explosive mechanisms to disperse their seeds, launching them away from the parent plant to reduce competition and increase the likelihood of colonizing new areas. These diverse strategies ensure that seeds are spread across a wide range of environments, increasing the chances of successful germination and growth.

Knowledge of floral structures and reproductive strategies has practical applications. In agriculture and horticulture, understanding plant reproduction is essential for cultivating and breeding crops. Techniques such as selective breeding, hybridization, and genetic modification are employed to produce plants with desirable traits, such as increased yield, disease resistance, or improved nutritional content.

Preserving pollinators and their habitats is critical for maintaining ecosystem health and productivity. Pollinators are responsible for the reproduction of many food crops and wild plants, and their decline poses a significant threat to biodiversity and food security. Conservation efforts aimed at protecting pollinators, such as creating pollinator-friendly habitats and reducing pesticide use, are essential for sustaining the intricate web of life that depends on these vital organisms.

In ecological restoration and conservation, understanding plant reproductive strategies can inform the management and recovery of degraded ecosystems. By selecting plant species with compatible pollination and dispersal mechanisms, restoration practitioners can enhance the resilience and diversity of restored habitats.

Floral structures and reproductive strategies are a testament to nature's ingenuity, showcasing the myriad ways plants have adapted to their environments to ensure survival and reproduction. Through the lens of plant reproduction, we gain a deeper appreciation for the complexity and beauty of the natural world, as well as the interconnectedness of all life forms.

The study of plant reproduction provides insights into evolutionary processes that have shaped life's diversity on Earth. By examining the relationships between plants and their pollinators, dispersers, and habitats, we uncover the intricate networks of interaction that drive evolution and sustain ecosystems.

Exploring the wonders of floral structures and reproductive strategies reminds us of the importance of preserving nature's delicate balance. By protecting plant diversity and their pollinators, we ensure the continued vitality of ecosystems that sustain us all. The story of plant reproduction is one of resilience and adaptation, inspiring and informing our efforts to live harmoniously with the natural world.

Symbiotic Relationships and Mutual Benefits

The natural world is a vast tapestry of interactions, where relationships between different species are as varied and complex as the ecosystems they inhabit. Among these interactions, symbiotic relationships stand out as particularly fascinating. These relationships, defined by close and often long-term interactions between different species, are a testament to the interconnectedness of life. They illustrate how different organisms, through cooperation and mutual support, can achieve survival and success in their respective environments.

Symbiosis can take several forms, but the most well-known is mutualism, a relationship where both parties benefit. This cooperative arrangement can be seen in numerous examples across the natural world, each showcasing the ingenuity of evolution in crafting alliances that enhance the survival and well-being of the involved species.

Consider the relationship between bees and flowering plants. In their quest for nectar, bees inadvertently transfer pollen from one bloom to another, facilitating the process of pollination. This mutually beneficial arrangement ensures that plants can reproduce, while bees obtain the nourishment they need. This relationship is not just a chance encounter but a finely tuned partnership that has evolved over millions of years, with flowers and bees adapting to each other's needs and preferences.

Another classic example of mutualism is the relationship between ants and aphids. Ants protect aphids from predators and parasites, and in return, they harvest the sweet honeydew that aphids produce. This exchange underscores the principle of mutual benefit that defines symbiotic relationships. Each participant offers something of value that the other cannot easily obtain alone, creating a bond that enhances their collective survival.

Symbiotic relationships can also be found in the ocean depths, where the vibrant colors of coral reefs are maintained by another type of mutualism. Corals house tiny algae within their tissues, providing them with a protected environment and access to sunlight. In return, the algae conduct photosynthesis, producing oxygen and nutrients that benefit the coral. This relationship is so critical that the health of entire reef ecosystems hinges on the well-being of these tiny partners.

Even in the soil beneath our feet, symbiosis plays a crucial role. Mycorrhizal fungi form partnerships with plant roots, extending their reach and increasing their ability to absorb water and nutrients from the soil. In exchange, the plant provides the fungi with carbohydrates produced during photosynthesis. This underground alliance boosts plant growth and resilience, illustrating how mutualistic relationships can drive the productivity of ecosystems on a fundamental level.

The benefits of mutualism are not limited to wild ecosystems; they also have practical applications in agriculture and horticulture. By understanding and harnessing these natural partnerships, humans can improve crop yields and sustainability. For instance, farmers may introduce beneficial insects like ladybugs to control pest populations, reducing the need for chemical pesticides. Similarly, incorporating nitrogen-fixing plants into crop rotations can enhance soil fertility and reduce the need for synthetic fertilizers.

In the realm of conservation, recognizing and preserving mutualistic relationships is crucial for maintaining biodiversity and ecosystem health. Protecting pollinators and their habitats, for example, ensures the continued reproduction of a wide variety of plant species. Similarly, efforts to conserve coral reefs must consider the intricate relationships between corals and their algal partners, as well as the myriad of other species that depend on these ecosystems for survival.

Symbiotic relationships also offer insights into the adaptability and resilience of life. These partnerships demonstrate how species can evolve in response to each other's needs, creating complex networks of interdependence. This adaptability is particularly relevant in the face of environmental changes and challenges, as mutualistic relationships can provide stability and support to ecosystems under stress.

However, mutualism is but one form of symbiosis. Other types include commensalism, where one species benefits without affecting the other, and parasitism, where one organism benefits at the expense of another. Each form of symbiosis highlights different strategies for survival and interaction, enriching our understanding of the natural world.

Commensal relationships can be seen in barnacles attaching to whales, gaining mobility and access to nutrient-rich waters while the whale remains unaffected. Parasitic relationships, such as those between ticks and their hosts, illustrate how one organism can exploit another for resources. These interactions, while different from mutualism, are equally important in shaping ecosystems and influencing the evolution of species.

The study of symbiotic relationships extends beyond biology, offering valuable lessons for human society. The principles of cooperation, mutual benefit, and interdependence that define these relationships can inform our approach to social, economic, and environmental challenges. By embracing the idea that collaboration and mutual support lead to greater resilience and success, we can foster a more harmonious and sustainable world.

In summary, symbiotic relationships reveal the intricate web of connections that sustain life on Earth. From the smallest microbes to the largest mammals, these partnerships demonstrate the power of cooperation and mutual benefit in overcoming challenges and achieving success. As we continue to explore and understand these relationships, we gain valuable insights into the resilience and adaptability of the natural world, inspiring us to cultivate similar principles in our own lives and societies. Through the lens of symbiosis, we see a world where collaboration and interdependence are not just strategies for survival, but pathways to thriving in a complex and ever-changing environment.

The Role of Plants in Soil Formation and Maintenance

The intricate relationship between plants and soil is a cornerstone of terrestrial ecosystems, playing a vital role in soil formation and maintenance. This dynamic interaction not only supports plant growth but also influences the broader ecological landscape. Plants, through their biological processes, contribute significantly to the development and preservation of soil, making them indispensable partners in the health of our environment.

Plants are among the primary architects of soil formation. Their roots, extending into the ground, interact with the underlying geological material, breaking it down into finer particles. This process, known as weathering, is facilitated by the physical and chemical actions of plant roots. As roots grow, they exert pressure on rocks, causing cracks and promoting fragmentation. This mechanical breakdown is complemented by chemical weathering, where root exudates—organic compounds secreted by roots—alter the mineral composition of rocks, further aiding in their decomposition.

The accumulation of organic matter is another critical aspect of soil formation. As plants grow, they shed leaves, stems, and other organic materials. This detritus accumulates on the soil surface, where it undergoes decomposition by microorganisms. The resulting organic matter, or humus, enriches the soil with nutrients and improves its structure. Humus enhances soil fertility by providing essential elements such as nitrogen, phosphorus, and potassium, which are vital for plant growth. Additionally, it improves soil moisture retention, aeration, and the ability to support a diverse microbial community.

Plants also play a crucial role in maintaining soil structure and preventing erosion. The root systems of plants act as natural stabilizers, anchoring the soil in place and reducing the impact of wind and water erosion. In areas where vegetation is sparse or absent, soil is more susceptible to being carried away by rainwater or blown away by the wind. This erosion can lead to the loss of fertile topsoil, diminishing the land's productivity and affecting the surrounding environment. By maintaining a robust cover of vegetation, plants help protect the soil from these erosive forces.

The interaction between plants and soil is not a one-way street; it is a symbiotic relationship where both parties benefit. Soil provides plants with essential nutrients, water, and a medium for growth. In return, plants contribute to soil health, enhancing its fertility and structure. This mutually beneficial relationship underscores the interconnectedness of life and the importance of maintaining healthy ecosystems.

In agricultural contexts, understanding the role of plants in soil formation and maintenance is crucial for sustainable farming practices. Crop rotation, cover cropping, and agroforestry are techniques that leverage the natural benefits of plants to improve soil health. Crop rotation involves alternating different types of crops in the same field to prevent nutrient depletion and reduce pest and disease buildup. Cover cropping, the practice of planting non-harvested crops like clover or rye, helps protect and enrich the soil during off-seasons. Agroforestry integrates trees and shrubs into agricultural landscapes, providing additional benefits such as shade, windbreaks, and enhanced biodiversity.

In addition to their role in agriculture, plants are critical in ecological restoration and land reclamation efforts. Reforestation and afforestation projects, which involve planting trees in deforested or barren areas, help restore degraded landscapes and improve soil quality. The deep roots of trees stabilize the soil, while their leaf litter adds organic matter, promoting nutrient cycling and enhancing soil structure. These efforts not only improve the ecological health of an area but also contribute to carbon sequestration, helping mitigate climate change.

The importance of plants in soil formation and maintenance extends to urban environments as well. Green spaces, such as parks, gardens, and green roofs, provide valuable ecosystem services in cities. They improve air quality, reduce urban heat, and manage stormwater runoff. Plants in urban areas also contribute to soil health by increasing organic matter and supporting biodiversity. The integration of plants into urban planning and design can lead to healthier, more resilient cities that are better equipped to handle environmental challenges.

While the role of plants in soil formation and maintenance is well-established, it is also subject to various threats. Deforestation, overgrazing, and unsustainable agricultural practices can disrupt the delicate balance between plants and soil, leading to soil degradation and loss of fertility. Climate change exacerbates these issues by altering precipitation patterns, increasing the frequency of extreme weather events, and affecting plant growth and distribution. Addressing these challenges requires a concerted effort to promote sustainable land management practices, conserve natural habitats, and mitigate the impacts of climate change.

The relationship between plants and soil is a testament to the interconnectedness of natural systems. By understanding and appreciating this relationship, we can develop strategies to protect and enhance soil health, ensuring the continued provision of essential ecosystem services. This knowledge is vital for addressing the global challenges of food security, biodiversity loss, and climate change.

In practical terms, individuals can contribute to soil health by adopting sustainable gardening practices, such as composting, mulching, and planting native species. Composting organic waste returns valuable nutrients to the soil, while mulching helps retain moisture and suppress weeds. Planting native species supports local biodiversity and ensures that plants are well-adapted to the local soil and climate conditions.

On a larger scale, policymakers and land managers can implement policies that promote sustainable land use and conservation. Incentives for farmers to adopt regenerative agricultural practices, protection of natural habitats, and restoration of degraded lands are critical components of a comprehensive approach to soil conservation.

The role of plants in soil formation and maintenance is a fundamental aspect of ecosystem health and resilience. By fostering a deeper understanding of this relationship, we can work towards a more sustainable and harmonious coexistence with the natural world. This endeavor is not only essential for the well-being of our planet but also for the future prosperity of human societies that depend on the services provided by healthy soils and thriving ecosystems.

Adaptations to Diverse Habitats and Climates

Adaptations in plants are a marvel of nature, demonstrating the intricate strategies developed over millennia to survive and thrive across diverse habitats and climates. These adaptations are not merely superficial changes but complex alterations that affect every aspect of a plant's physiology and structure. Understanding these adaptations offers insight into the resilience of life and the remarkable ways in which plants have mastered their environments.

Deserts, with their scorching temperatures and scarce water, pose one of the greatest challenges to plant life. Yet, species such as cacti and succulents have evolved remarkable adaptations to endure these harsh conditions. These plants often possess thick, fleshy tissues capable of storing water for prolonged periods. Their leaves, if present, are typically reduced to spines, minimizing surface area and reducing water loss. Photosynthesis is often modified, taking place primarily at night when cooler temperatures reduce evaporation, a process known as CAM (Crassulacean Acid Metabolism) photosynthesis.

In stark contrast, rainforests are lush, humid environments with intense competition for light and nutrients. Here, plants exhibit adaptations geared towards maximizing access to sunlight and efficiently utilizing available resources. Many rainforest trees develop broad leaves with drip tips that efficiently shed excess water, preventing mold and fungal growth. Lianas and epiphytes, such as orchids and bromeliads, have evolved to grow on other plants, reaching the canopy to access sunlight without expending energy on structural support.

Adaptations are equally impressive in temperate climates, where seasonal changes require flexibility and resilience. Deciduous trees, for instance, shed their leaves in autumn to conserve water and energy during the cold, resource-scarce winter months. By doing so, they also reduce the risk of damage from heavy snow accumulation. As spring arrives, these trees are quick to produce new leaves, taking advantage of the growing season.

In alpine environments, where temperatures are low and winds are fierce, plants like the alpine cushion plant exhibit a low, compact growth form that reduces exposure to the elements. This growth habit also traps heat and reduces water loss, critical adaptations for survival in such inhospitable conditions. Similarly, many alpine plants have a dark pigmentation, which absorbs more heat from the sun, aiding in temperature regulation.

Aquatic environments present their own set of challenges, and plants here have adapted in fascinating ways. In freshwater environments, plants like water lilies have broad, flat leaves that float on the water's surface, maximizing sunlight absorption for photosynthesis while allowing gas exchange. Their roots are anchored in the sediment, absorbing nutrients directly from the water. In saltwater environments, seagrasses have evolved to tolerate high salinity levels, using specialized cells to excrete excess salt.

Coastal habitats, frequently battered by salt spray and strong winds, are home to plants like mangroves that have developed unique adaptations. Mangroves thrive in saline, waterlogged soils by developing specialized root systems that provide stability and facilitate gas exchange. These roots, often visible above the ground, are crucial for oxygen intake in anaerobic conditions. Additionally, mangroves can excrete excess salt through their leaves, ensuring their survival in challenging coastal environments.

The evolutionary strategies employed by plants to adapt to cold climates are no less ingenious. In the tundra, plants such as mosses and lichens grow close to the ground, forming dense mats that resist cold winds and capture warmth from the sun. Their small, sturdy leaves are designed to minimize water loss, while their ability to photosynthesize at low temperatures allows them to make the most of short growing seasons.

The interplay of climate and habitat has also driven adaptations in plant reproductive strategies. In unpredictable environments, many plants produce seeds that can remain dormant until conditions become favorable. This dormancy ensures that germination occurs at the optimal time, increasing the chances of seedling survival. In fire-prone areas, some species have evolved serotiny, a trait where seeds are released in response to fire, taking advantage of the nutrient-rich ash bed left behind.

The study of plant adaptations extends beyond academic interest, offering practical applications in agriculture, conservation, and climate change mitigation. By understanding how plants have naturally adapted to extreme conditions, scientists and farmers can develop crops better suited to withstand droughts, floods, and other climate-related challenges. This knowledge is crucial as global climate patterns shift, presenting new challenges for food security and ecosystem stability.

Conservation efforts also benefit from insights into plant adaptations. Protecting plant species that have developed unique adaptations contributes to the preservation of biodiversity and the resilience of ecosystems. These species often play critical roles in their environments, supporting a wide array of wildlife and ecological processes. By conserving them, we maintain the delicate balance of nature and safeguard the services that ecosystems provide to humanity.

In horticulture, understanding plant adaptations can inform the selection of species for gardens and landscapes, ensuring that plants thrive in their intended environments. This knowledge allows gardeners to choose plants that are naturally suited to local conditions, reducing the need for artificial inputs such as water and fertilizers, and promoting sustainable gardening practices.

Adaptations to diverse habitats and climates underscore the versatility and ingenuity of plants. They reveal the myriad ways in which life on Earth has responded to environmental challenges, demonstrating the resilience and creativity inherent in nature. As we continue to explore and understand these adaptations, we gain valuable insights into the complexities of life and the potential for innovation in our own efforts to address environmental challenges.

The intricate dance between plants and their environments is a testament to the power of adaptation and the enduring will to survive. As we face global challenges such as climate change and habitat loss, the lessons learned from plant adaptations offer hope and guidance. By embracing the principles of adaptation and resilience, we can work towards a more sustainable future, where both humans and the natural world can thrive.

Human Impact on Plant Ecology and Diversity

Human activities have left an indelible mark on the natural world, profoundly affecting plant ecology and diversity. As the primary architects of environmental change, humans have altered landscapes, disrupted ecosystems, and introduced new challenges for plant species worldwide. Understanding the extent of this impact is crucial for developing strategies to mitigate harm and promote ecological resilience.

The expansion of urban areas, agriculture, and infrastructure has led to significant habitat loss and fragmentation. As cities grow and farmland expands, natural habitats are often cleared or transformed, reducing the available space for native plant species. This loss of habitat is one of the leading causes of biodiversity decline, as many plants are unable to adapt quickly enough to the changing conditions or migrate to more suitable areas. Fragmentation further compounds the issue by isolating plant populations, reducing genetic diversity, and limiting opportunities for reproduction and dispersal.

Pollution, in its various forms, poses another significant threat to plant ecology. Air pollution, particularly from industrial emissions and vehicle exhaust, can have detrimental effects on plant health. Pollutants such as sulfur dioxide and nitrogen oxides can lead to acid rain, which damages plant tissues, alters soil chemistry, and leaches essential nutrients from the soil. Ground-level ozone, a byproduct of air pollution, can also inhibit photosynthesis, reducing plant growth and productivity.

Water pollution, often resulting from agricultural runoff and industrial discharge, introduces harmful chemicals and nutrients into aquatic and terrestrial ecosystems. Excess nutrients, such as nitrogen and phosphorus, can lead to eutrophication, a process that depletes oxygen levels in water bodies and disrupts aquatic plant and animal communities. On land, contaminated water sources can affect plant health and survival, particularly in areas where water is scarce.

The introduction of invasive species, whether intentional or accidental, has significantly altered plant communities worldwide. Invasive plants, often free from their natural predators and diseases, can outcompete native species for resources such as light, water, and nutrients. This competition can lead to the decline or extinction of native plants, resulting in reduced biodiversity and altered ecosystem dynamics. The introduction of invasive plant pathogens and pests further exacerbates the problem, threatening both wild and cultivated plant species.

Climate change, driven by human activities, is perhaps the most pervasive threat to plant ecology and diversity. Rising temperatures, shifting precipitation patterns, and increased frequency of extreme weather events are reshaping ecosystems and challenging plant species' ability to adapt. Some plants may be able to migrate to more favorable environments, but many face barriers such as habitat fragmentation and limited dispersal capabilities. As a result, climate change may lead to shifts in plant distributions, changes in phenology, and increased vulnerability to diseases and pests.

Despite these challenges, humans have the power to positively impact plant ecology and diversity through conservation and sustainable practices. Conservation efforts, such as the establishment of protected areas and the restoration of degraded habitats, can help preserve plant species and their ecosystems. By protecting large, contiguous areas of habitat, we can safeguard biodiversity and promote ecological resilience.

Sustainable land use practices, including agroforestry, permaculture, and organic farming, offer ways to balance human needs with ecological health. These practices emphasize the integration of natural systems into agricultural landscapes, promoting biodiversity and reducing the environmental impact of food production. For example, agroforestry combines trees and crops in a way that enhances soil fertility, sequesters carbon, and provides habitat for wildlife.

Community involvement and education are also vital in promoting the conservation of plant ecology and diversity. By raising awareness of the importance of plants and the threats they face, individuals and communities can become active participants in conservation efforts. Local initiatives, such as native plant gardens and community reforestation projects, empower people to make a positive impact on their environment.

Policy and legislation play a crucial role in protecting plant diversity and promoting sustainable practices. Governments can implement policies that incentivize conservation, regulate pollution, and support research into plant ecology and biodiversity. International cooperation is also essential, as many environmental challenges, such as climate change and invasive species, transcend national borders.

In the face of daunting challenges, the resilience of plant species and ecosystems offers hope for the future. Plants have evolved over millions of years, developing strategies to survive and adapt to changing conditions. By supporting and enhancing these natural processes, we can foster ecosystems that are robust and capable of withstanding the pressures of a rapidly changing world.

As stewards of the planet, humans have a responsibility to safeguard the diversity and health of plant communities. By understanding the impacts of our actions and making informed choices, we can ensure that future generations inherit a world rich in biodiversity and ecological integrity. The journey towards a sustainable future requires collaboration, innovation, and a deep appreciation for the interconnectedness of all life.

The story of human impact on plant ecology and diversity is a complex narrative of challenges and opportunities. By acknowledging our role in shaping the natural world, we can embrace the responsibility of nurturing it. Through concerted efforts in conservation, sustainable practices, and education, we can pave the way for a future where both humans and plants flourish, coexisting in harmony with the environment.

Chapter 5: Plants and Their Environmental Interactions

The Impact of Light, Water, and Nutrients

The digital age has ushered in an era where cyber threats loom large over individuals, businesses, and governments alike. These threats, varied in nature and scope, pose significant risks to the security of personal data, financial assets, and even national infrastructure. Understanding the different types of cyber threats is crucial for developing effective defenses and safeguarding against potential attacks.

Phishing remains one of the most prevalent and insidious cyber threats, exploiting human psychology to deceive individuals into revealing sensitive information. Cybercriminals craft seemingly legitimate emails or messages, often impersonating trusted entities such as banks or government agencies. These communications typically contain malicious links or attachments designed to harvest personal data, such as login credentials or credit card numbers. Phishing attacks are constantly evolving, with perpetrators employing increasingly sophisticated tactics to bypass security measures and exploit unsuspecting victims.

Malware, short for malicious software, encompasses a wide range of harmful programs designed to infiltrate and damage computer systems. This category includes viruses, worms, Trojans, ransomware, and spyware, each with its unique methods of operation and impact. Viruses and worms replicate themselves to spread across networks, causing widespread disruption and data loss. Trojans masquerade as legitimate software, tricking users into installing them and granting unauthorized access to sensitive information. Ransomware encrypts a victim's files, demanding payment for their release, while spyware secretly monitors user activity, capturing keystrokes and other personal data.

Distributed Denial of Service (DDoS) attacks target the availability of online services by overwhelming servers with excessive traffic. These attacks are orchestrated using networks of compromised computers, known as botnets, which flood a target with requests until it becomes inaccessible to legitimate users. DDoS attacks can cripple websites, disrupt online services, and cause significant financial and reputational damage to organizations.

Advanced Persistent Threats (APTs) represent a more sophisticated and targeted form of cyber attack, often orchestrated by well-funded and skilled adversaries. Unlike other attacks that seek immediate gain, APTs aim to establish a long-term presence within a target's network, gathering intelligence and exfiltrating valuable data over time. These threats are particularly concerning for government agencies, corporations, and critical infrastructure operators, as they can compromise sensitive information and disrupt essential services.

Insider threats pose a unique challenge, as they originate from within an organization. Employees, contractors, or business partners with access to sensitive information may intentionally or inadvertently compromise security. Insider threats can result from malicious intent, such as theft or sabotage, or from negligence, such as failing to follow security protocols. Organizations must implement comprehensive security measures, including access controls and monitoring, to mitigate the risk of insider threats.

Social engineering attacks leverage human interaction to manipulate individuals into divulging confidential information or performing actions that compromise security. These attacks often involve impersonating authority figures or trusted contacts to gain the victim's trust. Social engineering can be conducted through various channels, including phone calls, emails, and even in-person interactions. As technology advances, attackers are increasingly using artificial intelligence and machine learning to enhance the effectiveness of social engineering tactics.

The Internet of Things (IoT) has introduced new vulnerabilities, as connected devices become an integral part of modern life. IoT devices, ranging from smart home appliances to industrial sensors, often lack robust security features, making them susceptible to hacking. Compromised IoT devices can be used to launch attacks, steal data, or disrupt services. As the number of IoT devices continues to grow, securing these devices against cyber threats is an urgent priority.

Supply chain attacks target the interconnected networks of suppliers and partners, exploiting vulnerabilities in third-party systems to gain access to a primary target. By compromising a trusted supplier, attackers can infiltrate the systems of multiple organizations, spreading malware or stealing data. Supply chain attacks highlight the importance of comprehensive security assessments and collaboration among organizations to protect against shared threats.

As cyber threats continue to evolve, organizations and individuals must remain vigilant and proactive in their defense strategies. Implementing robust cybersecurity measures, such as firewalls, antivirus software, and encryption, is essential for protecting sensitive information and systems. Regular security training and awareness programs can empower individuals to recognize and respond to potential threats, reducing the likelihood of successful attacks.

Collaboration and information sharing among governments, businesses, and cybersecurity experts are critical for staying ahead of emerging threats. By sharing threat intelligence and best practices, stakeholders can collectively enhance their defenses and respond more effectively to cyber incidents. Public-private partnerships can facilitate the development of innovative solutions and strengthen the overall cybersecurity landscape.

In conclusion, the diverse and ever-evolving nature of cyber threats demands a comprehensive and adaptive approach to cybersecurity. By understanding the various types of threats and their potential impact, individuals and organizations can implement effective strategies to protect against attacks and mitigate risks. As technology advances and the digital landscape becomes increasingly complex, the importance of cybersecurity cannot be overstated. Through vigilance, collaboration, and innovation, we can build a secure and resilient digital future.

Plant Responses to Environmental Stressors

Plants, like all living organisms, encounter a myriad of environmental stressors throughout their lifecycle. These stressors, ranging from drought and salinity to extreme temperatures and pollution, can significantly impact plant growth, reproduction, and survival. However, plants have evolved an impressive arsenal of responses and adaptations to mitigate the effects of these challenges, showcasing their resilience and ability to thrive in diverse environments.

Water scarcity, a common stressor in many regions, prompts plants to implement a series of physiological and morphological changes. Drought conditions trigger the closure of stomata, the tiny openings on leaves that facilitate gas exchange. By closing these pores, plants reduce water loss through transpiration, conserving moisture during periods of limited water availability. Additionally, some plants develop deeper or more extensive root systems to access water from deeper soil layers. Osmotic adjustment, where plants accumulate solutes like proline and sugars, helps maintain cell turgor and enzyme function under water-deficit conditions.

Salinity presents another formidable challenge, particularly in coastal and arid environments. High salt concentrations can disrupt cellular homeostasis and impair plant metabolism. To combat this, halophytes, or salt-tolerant plants, have developed specialized mechanisms to sequester excess sodium ions in vacuoles, preventing toxicity in the cytoplasm. Other plants synthesize compatible solutes, such as glycine betaine, to protect cellular structures and maintain osmotic balance. The production of antioxidant enzymes also helps mitigate oxidative stress induced by high salinity levels.

Temperature extremes, both hot and cold, necessitate adaptive responses for plant survival. In high-temperature environments, plants may produce heat-shock proteins that stabilize and refold damaged proteins, ensuring continued cellular function. Increased leaf reflectance, through the development of waxy or hairy surfaces, can reduce heat absorption and prevent overheating. Conversely, cold stress prompts the accumulation of antifreeze proteins and cryoprotectants, which stabilize cell membranes and proteins, reducing the risk of ice formation and cellular damage.

Heavy metal pollution, often a byproduct of industrial activities, poses significant threats to plant health. Metals such as lead, cadmium, and mercury can interfere with essential physiological processes. To cope, plants activate metal chelation and sequestration pathways, using molecules like phytochelatins and metallothioneins to bind and sequester metals in vacuoles. This detoxification process prevents metal ions from interfering with enzymatic activities and other cellular functions.

Plants also face biotic stressors, such as herbivory and pathogen attacks. In response to herbivore damage, plants may produce secondary metabolites like alkaloids, tannins, and terpenoids, which deter feeding and reduce palatability. Some species deploy volatile organic compounds that attract natural predators of the herbivores, effectively enlisting allies in their defense. Pathogen infection triggers the activation of the plant's innate immune system, leading to the production of pathogenesis-related proteins and the strengthening of cell walls through lignin deposition.

The intricate dance of plant responses to environmental stressors underscores the complexity and adaptability of plant life. These responses are not isolated events but part of an integrated network of signaling pathways that enable plants to perceive, respond to, and often overcome the challenges posed by their environment. The ability to adjust and thrive in diverse conditions is a testament to the evolutionary ingenuity of plants.

In agricultural settings, understanding plant responses to stressors is crucial for developing resilient crops that can withstand the challenges posed by climate change and resource scarcity. Breeding programs that focus on enhancing drought tolerance, salinity resistance, and temperature resilience are essential for ensuring food security in a changing world. Biotechnology also offers promising avenues for improving stress tolerance through genetic modification and the development of stress-responsive transgenic plants.

Conservation efforts benefit from insights into plant stress responses by identifying species and populations with inherent resilience to environmental challenges. Protecting these resilient species contributes to the stability and diversity of ecosystems, enhancing their ability to withstand disturbances and recover from adverse events.

For home gardeners and horticulturists, understanding plant responses to environmental stressors can inform practices that minimize stress and promote healthy growth. Selecting plant species suited to local conditions, providing adequate water and nutrients, and employing mulching and shading techniques can help mitigate the impact of stressors and support vibrant, resilient gardens.

The study of plant responses to environmental stressors is a dynamic and evolving field, revealing the myriad ways in which plants have adapted to the challenges of their environment. As research continues to uncover the molecular and physiological mechanisms underlying these responses, we gain valuable insights into the resilience of plant life and the potential to harness this resilience for the benefit of agriculture, conservation, and sustainable living.

In the face of increasing environmental challenges, the resilience of plants offers hope and inspiration. By understanding and supporting the natural processes that enable plants to thrive under stress, we can develop strategies to enhance the resilience of ecosystems and agricultural systems alike. This endeavor requires collaboration, innovation, and a deep appreciation for the complexity and adaptability of the natural world. Through these efforts, we can work towards a future where both plants and human societies flourish in harmony with the environment.

Mechanisms of Defense Against Herbivory and Disease

Plants exhibit remarkable resilience in the face of environmental stressors, having evolved a myriad of adaptive strategies to navigate challenges such as drought, salinity, temperature extremes, and pollution. These stressors can profoundly impact plant growth, reproduction, and survival, yet their ability to adapt and thrive underscores the incredible ingenuity of nature.

Water scarcity is a significant stressor that prompts plants to deploy various physiological and morphological changes to conserve moisture. Under drought conditions, many plants close their stomata, the tiny pores on leaves that facilitate gas exchange, to minimize water loss through transpiration. This adaptation, while conserving water, also reduces the intake of carbon dioxide necessary for photosynthesis, highlighting the delicate balance plants must maintain. Some species develop deeper root systems to access water from lower soil depths, while others accumulate solutes like proline and sugars to maintain cell turgor and enzyme function, ensuring survival during periods of water deficit.

High salinity levels, particularly in coastal and arid regions, present another formidable challenge. Salt-tolerant plants, or halophytes, have evolved mechanisms to sequester excess sodium ions in vacuoles, preventing toxicity in the cytoplasm. This adaptation allows them to maintain cellular homeostasis and continue metabolic processes despite high external salt concentrations. The synthesis of compatible solutes, such as glycine betaine, helps protect cellular structures, while antioxidant enzymes mitigate oxidative stress induced by salinity.

Temperature extremes necessitate distinct adaptive responses. In hot environments, plants produce heat-shock proteins that stabilize and refold damaged proteins, ensuring cellular function under thermal stress. Increased leaf reflectance through waxy or hairy surfaces reduces heat absorption, preventing overheating. Conversely, in cold conditions, plants accumulate antifreeze proteins and cryoprotectants to stabilize cell membranes and proteins, reducing the risk of ice formation and damage.

Heavy metal pollution, often resulting from industrial activities, poses significant threats to plant health. Metals like lead and cadmium can disrupt physiological processes, but plants have developed metal chelation and sequestration pathways. Molecules such as phytochelatins and metallothioneins bind and sequester metals in vacuoles, preventing interference with enzymatic activities and cellular functions, thereby detoxifying and protecting plant tissues.

Biotic stressors, including herbivory and pathogen attacks, elicit complex defensive responses in plants. To deter herbivores, plants produce secondary metabolites like alkaloids and tannins, which reduce palatability. Some species release volatile organic compounds that attract predators of the herbivores, enlisting natural allies in their defense. In response to pathogens, plants activate their innate immune systems, producing pathogenesis-related proteins and reinforcing cell walls to prevent further infection.

The intricate network of plant responses to environmental stressors is part of an integrated signaling system that enables plants to perceive and adapt to their surroundings. This adaptability is a testament to the evolutionary processes that have shaped plant resilience over millions of years.

In agriculture, understanding plant responses to stressors is crucial for developing resilient crops capable of withstanding climate change and resource scarcity. Breeding programs focused on enhancing traits such as drought tolerance and salinity resistance are vital for ensuring food security in a rapidly changing world. Biotechnology also presents opportunities to improve stress tolerance through genetic modification, creating transgenic plants that are better equipped to handle environmental challenges.

Conservation efforts benefit from insights into plant stress responses by identifying species and populations with inherent resilience. Protecting these species enhances ecosystem stability and diversity, improving their ability to recover from disturbances and maintain ecological balance.

For home gardeners and horticulturists, understanding plant stress responses informs practices that minimize stress and promote healthy growth. Selecting species suited to local conditions, providing adequate water and nutrients, and implementing techniques like mulching and shading can mitigate stress impacts and support vibrant gardens.

Research into plant responses to environmental stressors continues to reveal the underlying molecular and physiological mechanisms, offering valuable insights into plant resilience. This knowledge holds potential for agriculture, conservation, and sustainable living, highlighting the importance of supporting natural processes that enable plants to thrive under stress.

In the face of increasing environmental challenges, the resilience of plants offers hope and inspiration. By harnessing and enhancing these natural processes, we can develop strategies to bolster the resilience of ecosystems and agricultural systems alike. This endeavor requires innovation, collaboration, and a deep appreciation for the complexity of the natural world, paving the way for a future where plants and human societies flourish in harmony.

The Role of Plants in Carbon Cycling

Within the intricate web of Earth's ecosystems, plants assume a pivotal role in the global carbon cycle, a process essential for maintaining the planet's climate balance. Through photosynthesis, plants absorb carbon dioxide (CO_2) from the atmosphere and convert it into organic compounds, serving as a foundational step in the sequestration of carbon. This chapter delves into the mechanisms by which plants contribute to carbon cycling, highlighting their significance in regulating atmospheric CO_2 levels and mitigating the impacts of climate change.

The journey of carbon within the plant kingdom begins with photosynthesis, the process through which plants harness sunlight to synthesize glucose from carbon dioxide and water. This remarkable conversion not only forms the basis of plant growth but also acts as a natural mechanism for reducing atmospheric CO_2 levels. The glucose produced is used by plants for energy and growth, while excess carbon is stored in plant biomass, including leaves, stems, and roots. This storage capacity allows plants to act as carbon sinks, temporarily removing CO2 from the atmosphere and mitigating its greenhouse effects.

As plants grow, they continue to absorb carbon, incorporating it into their tissues and contributing to the accumulation of organic carbon in terrestrial ecosystems. Forests, in particular, play a crucial role in this aspect of carbon cycling. With their vast biomass, trees store significant amounts of carbon, both above and below ground. The dense networks of roots, trunks, and branches in forest ecosystems represent a substantial carbon reservoir, with mature forests often acting as stable carbon pools over long periods.

Yet, the role of plants in carbon cycling extends beyond photosynthesis and carbon storage. Plants also influence the decomposition process, wherein dead plant material is broken down by decomposers such as bacteria and fungi. This decomposition releases carbon back into the atmosphere as carbon dioxide, completing the carbon cycle. The rate and efficiency of decomposition are influenced by plant traits, including leaf composition and lignin content, which determine how quickly plant material is broken down. Plants, therefore, not only contribute to carbon sequestration but also regulate the timing and magnitude of carbon release back into the atmosphere.

In addition to terrestrial ecosystems, aquatic plants and phytoplankton play a significant role in carbon cycling within aquatic environments. Phytoplankton, microscopic plant-like organisms in oceans and freshwater bodies, are responsible for nearly half of the global photosynthesis. Through their rapid growth and reproduction, phytoplankton absorb vast amounts of CO2, which is then transferred through the aquatic food web. When these organisms die, their carbon-rich bodies sink to the ocean floor, where the carbon may be stored for long periods, effectively removing it from the immediate carbon cycle.

The interplay between plants and the carbon cycle is further influenced by land-use changes and anthropogenic activities. Deforestation, for example, reduces the capacity of forest ecosystems to sequester carbon, as trees are removed and carbon stored in biomass is released back into the atmosphere. Conversely, reforestation and afforestation efforts can enhance carbon sequestration, as newly planted trees absorb CO2 and contribute to the restoration of carbon sinks. Agricultural practices also impact carbon cycling, with techniques such as cover cropping and reduced tillage promoting soil carbon storage and improving soil health.

Understanding the role of plants in carbon cycling is crucial for developing strategies to mitigate climate change. By conserving and restoring plant-rich ecosystems, we can enhance their capacity to absorb and store carbon, thereby reducing the concentration of greenhouse gases in the atmosphere. Sustainable land management practices that prioritize biodiversity and ecosystem health can further bolster the resilience of these carbon sinks, ensuring their continued contribution to climate regulation.

Moreover, technological innovations inspired by plant processes hold promise for addressing climate challenges. Research into artificial photosynthesis and carbon capture technologies seeks to replicate and enhance the natural carbon sequestration capabilities of plants, offering potential solutions for reducing atmospheric CO_2 levels. These advancements highlight the importance of understanding and harnessing the inherent processes of the natural world to address environmental issues.

In the face of a changing climate, the role of plants in carbon cycling underscores the interconnectedness of Earth's systems and the critical importance of preserving biodiversity. By safeguarding plant ecosystems and promoting sustainable practices, we can support the natural mechanisms that regulate the planet's climate, fostering a more stable and resilient environment for future generations.

Ultimately, the intricate dance of carbon cycling, with plants at its core, is a testament to the delicate balance that sustains life on Earth. As stewards of the planet, it is our responsibility to recognize and protect the vital functions that plants perform within this cycle, ensuring that they continue to thrive and contribute to the health and stability of our world. Through collaboration, innovation, and a deep appreciation for the complexity of natural systems, we can work towards a future where the role of plants in carbon cycling is fully recognized and supported, offering hope and inspiration in the face of environmental challenges.

Adaptations to Extreme Environmental Conditions

Extreme environmental conditions pose significant challenges to the survival of living organisms, demanding remarkable adaptations and innovative strategies to endure and thrive. From scorching deserts to frigid polar regions, the natural world is a testament to the resilience and ingenuity of life. This chapter delves into the fascinating adaptations that have evolved in response to extreme environments, highlighting the diversity of strategies employed by various species to overcome the harshest of conditions.

In the relentless heat of desert landscapes, organisms face the formidable task of conserving water while enduring high temperatures. Many desert plants have evolved xerophytic adaptations that reduce water loss and maximize water uptake. Cacti, for instance, have modified leaves in the form of spines, which minimize surface area and reduce transpiration. Their thick, fleshy stems store water, allowing them to survive prolonged dry spells. Deep root systems enable these plants to tap into subterranean water sources, while their ability to open stomata at night, a process known as CAM (Crassulacean Acid Metabolism) photosynthesis, minimizes water loss during the hottest parts of the day.

Desert animals, too, exhibit remarkable adaptations. The fennec fox, with its large ears, dissipates heat efficiently, while its nocturnal lifestyle helps avoid daytime temperatures. Kangaroo rats have evolved to extract water from the seeds they consume, reducing their need for direct water sources. They also possess highly efficient kidneys that concentrate urine to conserve water. These adaptations underscore the intricate balance of physiological and behavioral strategies that enable survival in such arid environments.

In stark contrast, the polar regions demand adaptations to withstand extreme cold and limited resources. Polar bears, masters of the Arctic, possess a layer of blubber for insulation and a dense, water-repellent fur coat. Their large paws distribute weight when walking on thin ice, while their keen sense of smell allows them to detect prey beneath the snow. Similarly, Antarctic penguins have developed a unique huddling behavior to conserve heat, rotating positions within the group to ensure all members stay warm.

The plant life in polar regions is equally fascinating. Perennial plants like mosses and lichens have adapted to short growing seasons by entering a dormant state during the winter months and rapidly resuming growth as soon as conditions allow. These species have developed antifreeze proteins that prevent ice crystal formation within their cells, a crucial adaptation for surviving freezing temperatures.

High-altitude environments present their own set of challenges, where thin air and intense solar radiation require specialized adaptations. The Tibetan yak, for example, has adapted to the low oxygen levels of the Himalayas with larger lungs and increased red blood cell counts, enabling efficient oxygen transport. The colorful alpine flowers have developed ultraviolet-reflective pigments that protect against solar radiation while attracting pollinators.

In aquatic environments, species have evolved to cope with extreme pressures and darkness. Deep-sea creatures like the anglerfish use bioluminescence to lure prey, a vital adaptation in the pitch-black depths of the ocean. Their bodies are often soft and flexible, allowing them to withstand the immense pressure of the deep sea. The unique adaptations of these organisms showcase the remarkable diversity of life that thrives in even the most inhospitable corners of the planet.

The adaptability of life is not limited to the animal kingdom. Microorganisms, such as extremophiles, have evolved to survive in conditions once thought uninhabitable. Thermophilic bacteria flourish in boiling hot springs, while halophilic archaea thrive in highly saline environments. These microorganisms have adapted their cellular structures and metabolic processes to function optimally under extreme conditions, providing valuable insights into the potential for life beyond Earth.

Understanding these adaptations offers valuable lessons for human innovation and survival. Biomimicry, the practice of emulating nature's strategies, draws inspiration from these adaptations to develop technologies and solutions for modern challenges. From designing water-efficient agricultural practices inspired by desert plants to developing thermal insulation materials modeled after polar animals, nature's ingenuity continues to inform and inspire human endeavors.

Moreover, the study of adaptations to extreme environments underscores the importance of preserving biodiversity and protecting fragile ecosystems. As climate change alters environmental conditions worldwide, the resilience of species and ecosystems is increasingly tested. Conservation efforts must prioritize the protection of habitats and the preservation of genetic diversity to ensure that species can continue to adapt and thrive in the face of changing conditions.

In our quest to understand and appreciate the natural world, the adaptations of organisms to extreme environments serve as a powerful reminder of the resilience and creativity inherent in life. These adaptations not only highlight the incredible diversity of strategies employed by different species but also offer valuable insights into the interconnectedness of all life forms. By studying and preserving these adaptations, we can better

appreciate the complexity of the natural world and work
towards a future where both nature and humanity can
coexist and flourish.